M000303483

i

This book is dedicated to my mom.
She is the one that taught me to trust God
in every situation. She has helped me to
look at life through spiritual eyes.

THIS
IS
WHY
God's Plan Uncovered

TRIBUTE
PUBLISHING

2017

This is Why
First Edition June 2017

All Worldwide Rights Reserved
ISBN: 978-0-9982860-6-8

Instead of living through the fire of my hurt,
I lived according to my passion for Jesus Christ.

-    Jillian Murphy

CONTENTS

Introduction

Pain and hardships are not always easy to overcome. Waiting for the calm after the storm may seem more than we can bear. All of the trials and tribulations build upon us and we wonder why so much would be laid upon our shoulders. You may be sitting in a hospital next to a loved one, you may have just said goodbye to someone so close to you, and you may have experienced something that you don't believe anyone else will ever understand.

In other moments, we may experience what feels like the peak of our lives. Everything may be going the right way. The job you were working for, you may have gotten into, the school you applied to, you may have gotten in, and the prayer you have been praying for many years may have just been answered.

In all of these circumstances, the good and the bad, the easy and the difficult, the sorrow and the joy: God is in the midst of it all. God is in each moment and even when we reach what seems like our breaking point, He is there. When we reach higher than we ever dreamt possible, He is there.

So many times, I have heard so many questions of, "Why do bad things happen to good people? Why is this happening? How could this ever work for good?" These questions may not be directed at anyone, or may be directed at God. I have asked all of these questions at some point in my life. While asking these questions, I was so quick to forget all of the moments where we feel on top of the world, every instance where God has proven Himself. We tend to forget all of the times that life has gone our way and instead dwell in the pain we feel in the circumstance.

Many have heard the saying, "It will all work out for good." This book will prove that. All of these stories, I have personally experienced. These are personal encounters from my life where I didn't know if Christ could walk with me in this low of a situation and moments where His presence was overwhelming.

I have learned about God's true plan for our lives from this verse: "For I know the plans I have for you, declares the Lord, plans for welfare and not for evil, to give you a future and a hope" (Jeremiah 29:11 ESV). The Lord truly will make everything work out for the good. Now, this verse does not mean that all of the times in our lives will be happy and easygoing, but that one day we will see that He planned it all out for our welfare. This seems laughable if we are going through an immense hardship, but when truly broken down, you may be able to see it. You will look back upon your life and see all of the times that God truly was there for you. Even more so, one day you might see the purpose behind the pain.

I encourage you, if you ever reach the point where you see the purpose behind your pain or how God has worked in your life, to write it down. Write down all of the times God has proven Himself to you.

Then, when you are faced with something that seems impossible, go through each time God has proven Himself to you. Go through each moment and close your eyes and allow yourself to relive how you felt. Then, open your eyes and remember how great the God we serve is. Remember how you are still here today with a purpose. God has lead you through all of the struggles up until this point in your life, why wouldn't He deliver you now? Find a peace in the power of God.

While writing this, I know some of you will be able to relate to some of the stories, some will read this to be reminded of how great our God truly is, and others, to discover God for the first time. Please know that I am praying that the Lord uses this to work in each of your hearts. I believe that our God is all-powerful and I believe good will come of everything you have gone through. Do not brush over that statement. I believe and know for a fact that God can make good from ANYTHING. This seems like an overstatement at this point, but give God a chance, I promise you won't regret it.

Chapter One

A Dark Place

The room is quiet and the darkness has engulfed me. Tears have started to paint my face, telling all of the story that I cannot erase. My heart is heavy and my mind is full, all trying to understand the point and purpose of a God who was supposed to love me dearly. A God that is said to be my protector.

In the midst of the thick, quiet, and awful darkness, I hate. A hate that has never been openly described before. A hate that I could feel in every fiber of my being. A hate that crawls up and down my spine. A hate that cannot be erased, or at least a hate I thought could never be erased. A hate that pierces the soul of a joyful, pure child and leaves her empty. A promise of protection, of love, and trust; all broken over a repeated treacherous nightmare being lived over and over again for three years.

The nightmare wasn't a figure of the imagination, but was an action through a man. A man who hurt me. A man who made me feel ashamed and angry intertwined in one.

A man who invaded a space, invaded a private place, that was supposed to be saved. A man who could never take his actions back and a man that could never erase what had been done, but the hurt I will just have to carry on.

Many nights passed until the day came that everything was exposed to the light. Every hurt that I carried by myself for three years was now open to the light of day. The thing about sorrow being brought to the light is it forces you to feel the pain again, for everything that happened to be replayed in your mind over and over. Every hurt and fear come to light, and it is supposed to make you feel better. In reality, it crushes you a little bit more. In that time and that place, you feel like everyone is silently watching, judging, and waiting for you to break.

The courts seemed to diagnose my hurt, naming my nightmare: aggravated sexual assault. This word seemed so generic, like somehow the courts understood what happened to me. It was like I was now filed away in some group. I felt like the government had just placed me away from everyone else and stamped me with the red scar of victim, shut away and abandoned, to never come out.

The hurt I felt I saw reflecting back at me in my mother's eyes. She hurt. I will never know if in the moment that she found out if she could ever hurt like I hurt, but I saw it in her eyes. I saw the pain she began to carry of not knowing. She tried to understand, and I just tried to still be her little sunshine. As hard as I tried, I could not turn back into who I used to be; I didn't know her anymore. She was too far away now, lost in the oceans of lies and pain that I had to endure, barely keeping my head above water.

Chapter One: A Dark Place

Now that everything was in the light, I had to meet with child protective services. I didn't want to go, but I knew I had to. I knew there would be questions all over again. Questions that I did not want to answer. Questions that brought back too much, but I was there. I was ready to face whatever was next. I was so young, I didn't know how it could get any worse than this. I thought to myself, "I have faced all I have to face in my lifetime. God is not that cruel to put me through anything else."

I found myself walking into a room. One of the walls was a giant mirror, which I learned was actually one-way glass so others could listen to my conversation. In the room with me were two ladies facing towards me. These two ladies would not leave one stone unturned, not one memory left to rest. They kept asking me all of the details of every place and of every time. I just looked at them and started to become so angry. Every time? This made one tear fall, which was more than I ever wanted. I wanted to be strong; I never wanted to be seen as weak again. These women staring at me expected an answer to every time. My words trembled out, "I don't know how many times." This did not stop them. They still tried to get a definite number until they realized that my nightmare lasted for three years, I didn't know how many times.

When hurt comes to the light there is supposed to be a sense of relief, but this was excruciating. Why would you have me play this over and over again in my mind? Why do you keep asking me these questions? Why can't I go home? Being so young at the time, I just wanted to leave. Finally it was over, but I was completely unaware that the worst part was yet to come.

They told me that I did good. They just needed to talk with my family to see if they could put me in a support group with other children who were "like me." Like me? I thought, "I don't want to be labeled, I want this nightmare to be over, but everywhere I turn it just continues. I don't want to sit in a circle with other kids and hear who hurt them, how they did it, and how many times. I don't want to be set aside like I did something wrong. I just want to be normal again."

As I left the room, they told me I could choose a toy or a blanket to bring home with me. I started to look for a toy and I found a stuffed koala. The fluffy koala seemed to be special to me instantly. I didn't understand my connection, but nevertheless, I held it close to my heart. The lady came over and told me, "You have chosen a very special stuffed animal!" Excitedly, she pinched the arm of the koala. The koala then let out "I love you, I love you." I looked at the lady and back at the koala and knew my decision was made. I needed to know, even by this little koala, that I could still be loved. I had felt so alone for so long. Now with everyone knowing, I felt so disgusting. People kept asking me questions that I didn't want to answer. People kept looking at me and all I could feel was shame and an inner pain.

When we were about to leave, the lady pulled me aside. She told me that there was something I needed to do. She brought me over to a wall with a white piece of paper on it. All over it there were colorful hands of all sizes with a name and number. I looked at her and she told me, "Sweetie, you need to choose a color and we are going to put your hand up there, too." Immediately, I asked her, "Why?" And she was very honest with me, as she smeared paint all over my hand.

"Every hand on this wall represents a child that was molested just like you." I turned and saw the colorful hands and as I pressed my hand up against that white piece of paper, I realized that I was one of them. I was one of the many. A fire was ignited that day inside of me. I think a little of the childish innocence burned away. As I stood up and saw a wall full of hands surrounding me, I knew that the nightmare in my life happened in so many others lives. Walking away, the lady told me that the point of the wall was to let children know that they were not alone. I looked at her and walked away in silence.

It was almost better to have thought that this hurt that I was experiencing, only I was experiencing, but that idea was naive. The wall was living proof of how corrupt this world is and how truly awful it can be. Looking at how small some of those numbers were made a hole in my heart. This should never happen to anyone and the fact that there were so many was wrong. Beyond wrong, it was disgusting.

A little part of my childish joy was left there that day. I did not turn into an open activist or change my path at all. I was just so angry at life and I could never pinpoint it. I would get angry at a drop of a hat. Anything could set me off, and I knew it was a dark time for me, but I also knew that I did not want to confront it.

Then, one day I pressed my koala's arm and it said, "I love you, I love you." These simple words turned into a life-altering question. Looking back, I know it was not even as much of a question as it was a challenge, a challenge of Christ's love for me, a challenge if His intentions were good.

I asked God, "If you love me, why would you let this happen to me? Why would you let this hurt come upon my life? Why would you make me feel so dirty and worthless? Why would you allow this? What good could come of this? Why?" I knew that I was questioning God's plan for my life, but I truly wanted answers. I never truly thought I would gain an answer.

Chapter Two

Fire

We all face trials and tribulations. Whether it be earlier or later in life, we all have a storm to get through and a mountain to climb. Sometimes we find ourselves along the road and we are asking the question: Why? We dare to ask the Lord, "Why?"

This international plague of "why?" I have seen pouring out of the souls of people all over the world. I am blessed to have been on so many mission trips already in my life and one thing I hear in common everywhere to my question is, "Why do you not want to believe in Jesus?" the answer in return is always along the lines of, "How could a loving God allow... blank, blank, and blank happen in my life?"

Every time I hear those words, a little passion squeezes my heart so much I feel like I can feel their pain. I just want to reach out to them and hold them and tell them, "I don't know. I don't know why a loving God would allow this to happen to you, but we have to believe that it is for the good." This seems ridiculous for us to place hope in that the biggest struggle, that some of us may never speak aloud, has a purpose according to Christ's plan. This should not be taken lightly.

All of us have or will have a circumstance that will seem like it is impossible to overcome. Allow me to be the first one to tell you, it is. It is impossible for you to get through it alone, but with God on our side, nothing is impossible. What is impossible to us, is simple to God. He knows every day of our lives even before we are born. We try to fend for ourselves, while we have the option to ask God for help. God has the answer. He knows the solution to every problem we have if we just allow ourselves to bring it to Him. I originally believed this through blind faith and believed that God would just deliver me from anything. I believed that my God could do the impossible, but now I believe this because Christ has proven Himself to me.

A little later down the road, I met with a counselor. My family thought it would be a good idea for me to talk to someone about what happened. Like reliving it over and over in my brain would make something inside me hurt less, or talking would make my situation or label they had now placed on me disappear into the night air. The truth is, it doesn't. Nothing helps that I can see. Absolutely nothing. I sat in the counselor's office completely silent. She was supposed to be a specialist in this area. She was supposed to help me work through a lot of my hurt. We seemed to face off in our silence; she truly wanted to help and I truly did not want to speak.

When I sat silently, she told me, "It is okay if you don't want to speak." I continued to stare at her, it seemed like I had been staring at her for hours. She broke the silence and told me, "I have already talked with your mom. She has filled me in on everything. Tell me how you feel about it." I felt my stare transform into a glare, and so much anger that was buried within my heart resurfaced.

Chapter Two: Fire

Through all of the anger, I thought it was funny how this counselor, that I had known only for a few minutes, thought she knew everything. How could anyone think they knew, or even understood, everything? I kept thinking, silently, "How do you know how I feel if you have never walked in my shoes? You were not there. No one was, except for him." But my lips might as well have been sealed shut and my eyes daggers as I continued to sit silently.

What felt like a lifetime later, the session was finally almost over. She looked me over and she slowly spoke the words, "Jillian... we only have a few minutes left together." Still sitting silently, she continued to tell me all of the cliché notions of how I am not alone. This phrase made me so angry. I don't understand why people keep telling me this. I don't know if somehow knowing that this horrible nightmare happening to more than just me is supposed to help in any way, but it doesn't. She hit the wrong button without even knowing it. She continued to talk, but all I could imagine were those colorful hands plastered all over the wall representing each child, racing the words "I am not alone," over and over in my head. I hated the thought of anyone hurting like I did, and the anger just continued to grow in my heart.

I came back into the moment and saw her lips moving, realizing I wasn't hearing a word she was saying. She continued on, looking at me with urgency, "Just know... that you are not alone. Sometimes it just helps to know that." The way she said this made me realize she does not know what exactly to say, but she is willing to help. My anger should not be centered on her. All she is doing is trying to help.

The moment in which my anger started to calm was very small. I still don't know why she would ever tell me all of the probabilities of "victims," but she did. She started to explain that the probability of me doing well without talking about what I went through is very slim. It was like she had just attacked me and I didn't even see it coming. Her lips continued to move, as she began to read statistic after statistic about children who have been molested. Some never graduate high school, commit suicide at an early age, girls become teenage mothers, and so on. I sat dumbfounded. How dare she? How dare she act like she knows me. She has no idea who I am or what I am capable of. I took those words and bundled them inside me, each statistic to me was a challenge to exceed them from this day forward.

Leaving the office that day, I told my mom that I never wanted to go back. I knew I would never go back, but I also knew I would never let her be right about me. Her words and all of the statistics never left my brain. The thought that she was going to continue to label me and see me as a "victim" was the last straw. I knew that I would defy every statistic she listed. I would be great. I will not be a statistic. I decided to be great not because I wanted to be, but because I wanted to defy the expectation set of me by the world.

Chapter Three

Unconditional Love

Striving to defy every statistic, I continued life. I made sure to keep everyone and their help at arm's length. I didn't want to hear about going back to any more counseling sessions. I did not want to hear about what might help. I just wanted to make it. Where exactly I was trying to make it to, I had no idea. All I knew was that I would not become who they assumed.

My hurt continued to consume me. Sometimes in life, we have this perceived notion that if we run hard enough, we may just escape all of our problems. Well, this is not true to any extent. We cannot run from our problems, but with Christ's help, we can confront them. This is the point I had to come to. The point of healing. The point of accepting that I have run my race hard enough alone and have nothing to show for it.

I was actively involved in church and church activities, but nothing hit me to the core. A part of my heart still had an enormous void that could not be filled. For such a long time, I was trying to fill it by chasing success. I found out soon enough that no amount of A's, positions, or achievements could fill the void.

11

Stuck in my cycle, I kept living like this. Then, I went to a weekend retreat with my church. This retreat had all that I was used to, all of the fun worship songs and friends surrounding me. I went through the weekend exactly how I went through every day, just going through the motions. The speaker came up on the last night and it was like the whole room disappeared.

Looking up at the stage, only the two of us existed. He looked at me and told me how some of us may have a shame upon our life. A hurt that is unspeakable. All of a sudden, I felt myself choke up. It was like my hurt just arose and jumped to my throat. He continued on to let me know that all of my hurt was not meant to be carried on my own. This statement was what I was missing all along. It was not meant to be carried by me. My hurt, shame, guilt, and pain was not my burden.

A warmth rushed all over my body as I just looked up and said, "Okay, Father. I'll give it to you." Tears flowed from my face as I walked up to the front of the church. So much pain that was built up inside of me started to rush out of me. All the tears were pouring out like I had never allowed myself to cry out loud. I knew I was accepting Jesus Christ into my heart that day. I was asking the Lord to help me.

The next morning, there seemed to be a clean slate for my life. My heart seemed to have been emptied out. I was ready to start new. I wanted to start off by reading my Bible, and the night before was confirmed as I read: "For I, the Lord your God, hold your right hand; it is I who say to you, 'Fear not, I am the one who helps you'" (Isaiah 41:13 ESV).

The warm rush came back, as I felt the Lord speaking to me clearly. God did not intend for me to be carrying this burden on my own.

As I closed my eyes to pray, I pictured myself as a little girl, thinking of all the pictures of a huge, pure smile across my face. Then, I saw myself grasping the hand of someone right beside me and walking in the white nothingness. I realized this is the way it is supposed to be. I need to have a childlike faith. Not a blind one that denies hurt and pain, but a childlike one. A child that holds tightly to the hand of her Eternal Father. A little girl who has no worry or fear of what is to come because it is not her place. My place was to give my burden to the Lord, my place was to look to God and know He is here to help me.

Opening my eyes to face the day, I felt different. I did not feel the void anymore. The void that I was carrying for such a long time was gone. I realized that the Lord filled it. The void formed because I was trying to live life on my own away from my Eternal Father. I was trying to continue my life on my own and I could not attain it all. But when I turned to the Lord, my void was filled. The Lord took my hand and showed me that He was here all along ready to help. I just had to let Him in.

The feeling of coming to Christ is one that you will never forget. I will never forget how, for the first time in years, I felt like I was going to be okay. I knew I didn't have to hold everything together for show anymore. I left my burdens at the cross. I gave them to God for Him to handle for me. After the day I accepted Christ into my life, I was not perfect.

I would try to go back and take my burdens back, but I learned to actively trust in Him. I trained myself to actively acknowledge that I failed on my own and need Christ.

The need for Christ in my life began to grow. It went from a dutiful need to a full-blown passion. I had fallen in love with Christ. Fallen in love with the way He rescued me. How he loved me in all of my filth. How the warmth surrounding me was His hug placed upon me. He was holding me. I loved the way I felt safe in His presence. Jesus loved me with His unconditional love. I fell in love with Jesus Christ. And I keep falling in love with Jesus.

My passion for Christ started to cover the fire placed in my heart so long ago. Everything was not okay, but for the first time in a long time, I saw the light at the end of the tunnel. I saw a hope in the future and that was good enough for me. Instead of living through the fire of my hurt, I lived according to my passion for Jesus Christ.

I had a longing in my soul that wanted to tell everyone of how the Lord had set me free from my hurt. A part of me could not keep quiet about Jesus. As the passion grew inside of me, I went to my mom. I told her that I was ready to go on a mission trip. I had heard about them growing up but never felt the urgency to go. For a while in my life, I went through the motions of a Christian life, but I was missing the whole purpose. In that moment, I knew the orientation of my heart solely lied within the Lord. Beyond anything else, I wanted to tell people about Jesus, I wanted to actively share my faith.

My mom directed me to the Great Commission (Matthew 28:16-20 ESV). She pointed out to me that I could start today. I could share my faith in my everyday life. I did not need to leave the country or even my own zip code to have the opportunity to share my faith with someone. I could share with someone of God's unconditional love right where I was. From that day forward, I knew that for such a time as this, my school hallways were my mission field.

I began to pray continuously to be able to have gospel-centered conversations. As I began to tell people about Jesus and began to listen to their stories, I realized how hurt people are and how God can save. Buried deep within myself, I prayed to meet one of the kids that had their handprint painted on that wall with mine. I wanted to see where they were and how they were doing. I was eager to share with them that I found the key. I found the answer to all the questions I cried at night alone. I found the fulfillment to my void. I wanted them to find Jesus, just like I had.

Deep down, I knew the only thing that was keeping my life together was Jesus Christ. Because of that, I felt the need to tell as many people about Him as possible. I was presented with various opportunities to start going on mission trips with my church. On the trips, I had countless opportunities to share the gospel of God's unconditional love. The more people I talked to about Christ, the more I prayed that I didn't go through my hurt for nothing.

A trend was brought to the forefront of my mind as I talked to people about their prayer requests. I realized that most of the time, there was a substantial hurt keeping them from Christ. I truly wanted to hear their reasoning of not wanting to come to Christ, not from an argumentative standpoint, but to truly understand their outlook on life. I wanted, in each conversation, to be able to see from their perspectives, even if just for those few minutes. Finally, I began to understand, no one had the same reasoning for not loving Jesus. The majority of people either were already Christians, held on to their own belief system strongly, never thought of a belief system, or, what hurt me the most… they felt there was an obstacle between them and Jesus.

This realization was like I spotted an invisible wall between God and these people. Each person's wall was different but substantial enough to keep them away. I knew that my wall was being hurt for those three years. Also, I knew that I was not able to overcome that wall on my own. Only by Christ Jesus did I get through and I am still working through that pain. I started to pray that everything that I went through wasn't for nothing. This prayer seems meaningless to some, but to me, it meant the entire world. I wanted to know beyond a doubt that I served a loving God. That I have a passion for a good God. I didn't want to be naive, thinking everything is always rainbows and sunshine. I just wanted to truly know that every wall that we face has purpose. That every wall can be broken down with Christ by our side, and when we finally break down our personal wall, one day we might meet someone that is faced with a similar wall. Then, we will have the answer on how to help them tear down their wall as well.

Instantly, I knew after I prayed that one day I would find my one person. I would be the person to see their wall, pinpointing the person that knows what it feels like to feel so dirty, to feel like they do not want to make eye contact with anyone because of the shame they carry. One person that I could hold and tell them, 'I don't know why God would allow this, but I know that it will work out for the good.' I want to be able to direct at least one person to scripture and allow Jeremiah 29:11 to wash over them. "For I know the plans I have for you, declares the Lord, plans for welfare and not for evil, to give you a future and a hope."

Hearing this verse, I prayed that they would realize that God loves them. He did not wish to cast an immeasurable burden upon each of our lives to keep us from Him. God allowed Satan to place trials in our life, but He has every intention of having us walk through the trial with Him by our side. I wanted to be able to encourage my one person and help myself fully believe that everything does work out for the good. I knew that one day I would meet the one person that I could share my journey with. The one person that would help me understand some of the pain I went through.

Chapter Four: The Call

Chapter Four

The Call

My life continued on as I prayed to meet my one person. I still had a passion for sharing the gospel and the summer before my junior year was the summer that changed everything. Through my church choir, we went to Washington, D.C. This mission trip was life changing to say the least. Our choir gave concerts where we were able to sing and dance, then go and tell people about Christ. I loved how we could use our talents to magnify Christ's name and share the gospel. Outside of the concerts, our choir was so large that we were separated into groups. The groups all had different service projects. During the day, we would serve at our location before our concerts in the evenings.

My group was assigned to Central Union Mission, a men's homeless shelter. My passion for ministry grew as I served there alongside my group. As we cleaned bathrooms, rooms, the kitchen, and served food, I began to dwell on how there was something different about serving here. There was something about the homeless population in Washington, D.C. that caught my eye. As I served the men food, they began to ask me "Why do you think we are homeless?" Why I thought they were homeless? I had no idea. My mind immediately raced through all of the possibilities.

I began to think of how sometimes, back home, people would tell us not to give money to people who are homeless because they will go buy drugs and alcohol. I asked them, "Did it have anything to do with drugs or alcohol?" The men began to laugh at me. They were not even angry, they wanted to prove to me how close-minded people can live if they do not choose to examine life outside of their own perspective. The men began to explain each of their stories of how they got to Central Union Mission. Some of the men went through a nasty divorce and lost everything. Others went bankrupt trying to do all of the right things. I never thought of any of these reasons until I met these men. As I continued to talk to the men, I began to wonder, how much more of life was I closing myself off to?

Each day I woke up on the mission trip, I woke up excited to help in any way possible. I was excited to hear more stories from the men and broaden my perspective. One specific day, when we were walking to the men's homeless shelter, our choir gave us boxed lunches. Our group decided to give away our boxed lunches to people that seemed to need them. Then, we would grab lunch somewhere before the concert. I loved the idea to do a little good before getting to the homeless shelter.

As our group walked, our group leaders reminded us to stay together. We all knew the rule to stay together and it seemed simple. I was walking with the group and could not find anyone to bring my boxed lunch to. No one seemed to truly need it. Then, my eyes locked with this middle-aged woman. She had a ginormous suitcase that was standing above half of her body. We were only a few blocks away from a train station, so it didn't seem odd. She was standing there and seemed like she knew what she was doing.

Then, I felt the Holy Spirit telling me, "Give your boxed lunch to her." I tried to shake it. I did not want to give the boxed lunch to her, she was not homeless. She may be waiting on a bus or catching a train and I did not want to bother her. The Holy Spirit continued to prompt me until I walked straight over to her.

Walking up to her, I stood face to face with her and had not thought of one thing to say yet. Now that I was close to her, I could see that her clothes seemed dirty and very worn out. I looked at her and my mouth seemed to just open, "Hi, my name is Jillian. I am on a mission trip with my church choir from Dallas, Texas. I was wondering if you would possibly want this boxed lunch." There seemed to be a long pause as she stared at me in awe. She seemed to snap out of it and began to thank me over and over. She offered me a place to sit beside her on the curb as she began to eat the boxed lunch. While eating, she told me how much of a blessing I was because she did not know where she was going to get her next meal. She told me that she lived out of her suitcase and on the streets. I immediately saw that God led me to her because I did not even know she was homeless.

I learned that her name was Jane and as she ate her food, we continued to talk. I told her that my group and I were serving at Central Union Mission, a men's homeless shelter, and she did not seem to take this the best way. She started to visibly become defensive and I asked if I said something to offend her. She told me how often she hears of groups going to men's homeless shelters and how there are countless men's homeless shelters, but there are almost never any women's shelters. I asked her why there were more shelters for men than for women.

Instantly, I recognized that I asked her the golden question. She started to pour out to me. She told me how ridiculous it was that there are not many women's shelters around. She said the few that are around, you have to get there before a certain time, but if you want to get a job, your job usually doesn't allow you to leave until after that time, and then all the rooms have been filled. Then, if you don't have a job, you can get in line for the shelter earlier to hopefully get a room. But when there are only a few rooms left, there are often fights over who will get into the shelter. She looked at me like she was trying to teach me everything she knew in a short period of time.

She told me how the streets aren't made for women to survive. Eventually, all women become prostitutes to help themselves survive or they end up dead. Her reality burst my bubble that I was living in. I thought I understood so much, but in reality, I had no idea. I never thought of prostitution as a means to survive. I asked her what she did to survive. She told me that she fights to get a bed but some nights she can't. She told me about one specific night, not too long ago.

Jane looked away from me and I could see the shame that was rushing over her. She told me how a man approached her. A man came to her with a hotel key. He told her the hotel and the room number and the exact time to meet him. She told me that she shut him down quickly. She would never sell herself like that. But then she began to rationalize what she decided to do. He asked her when was the last time she was able to take a hot shower? Or had a decent meal to eat? Jane continued to turn further away from me as she continued on with her story. She told me how his offer seemed to be worth it. She knew exactly the price to pay for it, but it seemed worth it at the time.

Finally, with tears running down her face, she told me that she slept with him for the food, shower, and shelter. She could barely speak, her tears were running down her face, ashamed of what she had done. Instinctively, I scooted closer to her and held her in my arms, just holding her and rubbing her back. When I let go of her, I lifted her head and asked if she knew about Jesus. I asked her if she knew of my God who loves us unconditionally. She told me that He doesn't know all that she has done. And I told Jane, He knows everything. God knows you by name and even knows everything about both of us. He loves each of us. I continued on to point out that God does not want us to earn His love. The price was already paid as Jesus died on the cross for our sins and rose again on the third day.

Jane began to smile through her tears. I asked her does she believe a God could love her unconditionally? And she let out a broken yes. I asked her if she wanted to walk with me through accepting Christ into her heart. Then, more confidently, she said yes. That moment Jane became a Christian. I gave her a Bible and the cash out of my wallet and promised to pray for her.

As I walked away from Jane, I realized that I did not see my group. I could not see the leaders or any of the students anywhere. Then, I started walking towards the shelter, saw my leader with some of the students and police officers, and immediately wondered what could have happened. When they saw me, they came running to me and asked me where I had been. I was so confused as to why they were so worried.

One of the leaders continued to talk on the phone. I heard her say, "Yes, we found her. Yes, you can talk to her." The phone was passed to me.

I said, "Hello?" and the voice on the other end was my mom. She started to cry and she cried to me, "Jillian... what did I tell you about leaving the group? Are you okay? What happened?" In that instant, I realized I had been missing for hours. What seemed to be a very quick conversation was actually me being missing for hours. I explained to my mom that I was giving a homeless woman my boxed lunch, then I talked with her and led her to Christ. My mom told me that she was glad that God was using me, but I could not wander away from the group. I told her I would be very careful and it would not happen again. My leaders started talking with me and asked me why I would stay and talk with the lady, and words immediately flew out of my mouth. "I knew I was safe." The words even startled me. My mind raced back to my conversation with Jane. I remembered looking away from the conversation and seeing one of my leaders standing at a distance and continuing talking with Jane. He then explained to me that it was impossible that I saw him because they looked all over the homeless shelter for me.

God wanted me there. I knew without a doubt that God wanted me there to speak with Jane for a reason. He wanted me to have the conversation with Jane and feel completely safe. The police officers told me that they were glad I was safe, but I needed to be more careful. They asked me where exactly I was and they told me that I was very lucky. My leaders and I asked the officers, "Why?" The police officers continued to tell us that I was on a corner of a very prominent gang in the area. They always meet just right around the corner from where Jane and I were. The officers told me I was lucky that they didn't see me alone with just another woman. I knew luck had nothing to do with it.

Christ had placed me there for a reason and the reason that instantly came to my mind was so that Jane would become a believer and I could talk to her boldly without fear of my surroundings. I would later learn that there was so much more than that.

As the leaders continued to tell me about how worried everyone was, I was just amazed at the power of Christ. In gang territory and missing, I was talking with Jane and being used as a vessel to talk with her about Jesus Christ. I told the leaders about my experience and they immediately began to praise the Lord of how great God is.

In the midst of what was a happy moment, a phrase of what Jane said burned into my mind: how women on the streets end up in prostitution or dead. I hated those odds. Those odds seemed stacked up against Jane exactly how they were stacked up against me. I felt the fire inside me that I thought was silenced, burning inside me once again.

That night, we had a worship session and prayer time. The odds stacked up against the women on the streets kept tossing around in my heart and I couldn't shake it. As the worship leaders began to sing "Oceans" by Hillsong, everything became clear to me. God wanted me there so that I could talk with Jane about Christ, but also so that I could hear the pain of the women on the streets firsthand. Jane impacted me as much as I impacted her that day. As I sang and worshipped the Lord, I felt God speaking to me loud and clear. As we sang the words, "Take me deeper than my feet could ever wander, so that my faith would be made stronger in the presence of my Savior," I felt a tug on my heart. Throughout everyone praising, a voice was telling me to follow a path into women's ministry.

My answer immediately and out loud was no. No, I wanted a path where I could live comfortably and not worry about money. I wanted the easy way out. Right when I started hearing my excuses, I heard God's answer that I was supposed to be the person to show women that there was a third option. Christ. Jesus can rescue anyone and we do not need to clean ourselves up before we come to Him, we can come to Him just how we are. I looked up and started crying and saying yes. I knew that my life was going to change and that I needed to start following God's calling on my life immediately. I was now going to allow women on the streets to know that Jesus Christ is their third option and they can come to Him exactly how they are.

Chapter Five

Grace Packages

After my call to ministry, I knew I wanted to follow in immediate obedience. I wanted to take action to follow what I believed my purpose was: to help women off the streets. Now, in my junior year of high school, I was part of a program called Independent Study and Mentorship. The program helped students find a mentor in their future field and learn about the field before going to college. Along with a mentor, the students would have to complete an original work and final product.

I knew after my mission trip in Washington, D.C. that I wanted to study something to do with helping women off the streets. I had no idea what field I was pursuing or who would even be a possible mentor for me. I began to pray that the Lord reveal to me my mentor. I began the process of cold calling various professionals and asking them for informational interviews. Through the program, I was able to interview so many amazing people working with hurting men and women through halfway houses, counseling, and support groups.

Everyone I interviewed was following their unique calling from the Lord, but it seemed as if mine did not align with anyone else's. There were so many worthy causes and hurting people that I began to question the validity of my calling. I began to question if I had even had that specific of a call to ministry. Then, I called my friend's mom who worked with women on the streets and I just wanted to hear what she did.

When I met with her, she told me of all of the stories of women on the streets that she has had the opportunity to help. She told me of the hope they gained through this safe house and how their lives completely turned around for the good. All that was flowing from her mouth was my EXACT calling. There were so many worthy causes in need of help, but she hit mine on the bullseye. I was reassured that the Lord had a mentor out there for me. I began to ask her what safe house she led her Bible study at. She told me Restored Hope Ministries.

She put me in contact with the Chief Executive Officer of Restored Hope Ministries. I told him that I would like to meet with him for an informational interview. He said yes. That yes turned into a full-blown mentorship for me. I realized then that I would never need to settle while following the will of God. If God has called me to do something, He will provide a path for me to accomplish the goal set in front of me. I just have to faithfully follow Him.

After my call to ministry, I prayed continuously for the women on the streets. I prayed for Jane, that she would find a way out of the cycle. I desperately wanted to do something to save the women. I wanted to become the Chief Executive Officer of my own company that helps women off the streets, possibly through a homeless shelter exactly like

Central Union Mission. Central Union Mission had an optional program to disciple men, get them a job, and the first steps to getting off the streets. I wanted to create a version of the homeless shelter for women. Restored Hope Ministries was the closest place to what I could see myself running in the future. The only difference was that Restored Hope Ministries was a safe house.

Restored Hope Ministries had a select amount of women. The women came from all different backgrounds, but all were seeking help. The CEO said something that I never will forget on the first day I met him: "You can't help someone that doesn't want help." He was referring to the women they brought into the safe house. The women come from backgrounds of sex trafficking, prostitution, drug addiction, and domestic violence. The CEO and his wife created a year to a year-and-a-half long program for these women to go through. In the program, they are taught basic computer skills, have Bible studies, and take art and dance classes. The program helps them find a job after they have been in the program for a certain length of time. The women who go through the program have the ability to take their lives back, and the day I interviewed at the safe house, I fell in love with the program.

As a part of my high school program, I asked The CEO to become my mentor, which he graciously agreed too. I came at least once a week and did whatever needed to be done. My favorite thing to do was to just talk to the women. I was so young, so many of them had children near the same age as me. They were very open with me about their past and about their willingness to get their lives back. Many of them talked to me about how they were homeless at a certain point in their journey. Homeless women came back into the forefront of my mind. From my original calling, I had moved from wanting a homeless shelter to a safe house. I still wanted to make a tangible impact on the homeless community in my area. The question started to burn into my mind of how I could make the impact on the homeless population in this area.

This question became my driving motivation behind my proposed original work. I could not think of anything original to impact my field. So many people always say they want to change the world, but how does change start? I sat down and just started listing out what the women kept telling me about being homeless for a certain extent in their lives. This thought set a lightbulb off in my brain. I remembered, as a little girl, telling my mom that I would throw a huge concert and to get in you would have to donate care packages to the homeless. Then after the concert, we would go out and deliver the care packages to the homeless population.

The idea was so pure, I knew I could do it when I was so young. Why couldn't I use that idea now? There is a need that needs to be met, so why can't I help meet it? I proposed the idea to my Independent Study and Mentorship teacher, but instead of a concert, I would create and sell t-shirts and cold call businesses asking for their donations with the packages. The proposal was approved and the idea gained wheels. I was ready to accomplish a dream I had placed my mind to when I was so young.

As I began my project, I started off with trying to create a logo for the t-shirt design. I never thought of how much work it would actually take into placing together a design and having to sell the shirts. Also, the concept of cold calling companies never scared me, but the rejection hurt. I never thought of being turned away or turned down. I knew how much I believed in my project and I assumed that everyone else would as well.

I realized then, after so many no's from various different companies, that this task could not be done on my own. I was trying to complete everything by myself by the grit of my teeth. I was so wrong and so naive. I cannot, and no one can, make it through this world by the grit of their teeth. We have the help from God and I had not turned to Him in a long time. I didn't even pray over the project. I just thought my hard work would suffice and make everything come together. But on the contrary, I needed Him more than ever. That was the day I sat down and listed out everything I wanted in my packages and everyone I would call for donations. Then, I began to pray over the project. Until that point, I thought of calling the packages, homeless care packages. I knew after praying that these were not just homeless care packages, they were "Grace Packages." 2 Corinthians 12: 9 became my mission statement from that day forward: "But he said to me, 'My grace is sufficient for you, for my power is made perfect in weakness.' Therefore, I will boast all the more gladly of my weaknesses, so that the power of Christ may rest upon me." This verse reminded me that not by my power and my esteem will I get anywhere, but by God's grace that He may favor me and use me as a vessel to help others. I will never be enough, but by the power of Christ, He will make me more than enough.

After praying, the t-shirt orders came flowing in and the donations as well. Everything that could not be donated I bought with the money and I had to the exact cent what I needed to make Grace Packages happen. I knew I wanted to pass them out in the Dallas area and so I looked up homeless shelters to find an area with a high homeless population.

I had all the donations together, but I knew that this wasn't enough. In the packages we had soap, shampoo, conditioner, lotion, socks, a toothbrush, toothpaste, a granola bar, and a water bottle, but still there was something missing. Then, I remembered it is not by my strength alone. There is something that cannot be filled just by possessions. We all have a God-shaped hole in our lives, and only God can fill it. I knew the package would be a blessing to anyone, but the blessing would only be temporary. There was no eternal impact from a bag filled with groceries because when they finish everything in the bag at the end of the day, they will still have a God-shaped hole inside of them. I knew that my mission was so much farther than just the temporary. So, I began my search for Bibles.

While placing together the packages, I knew I needed Bibles. With each bag that I placed together, I knew it would help their physical need, but I wanted so much more than that. I wanted the package to help make an eternal impact, to plant a seed in someone's life. I may never get to see any of the people again who are given these packages, but one day God may use this blessing to show them that He truly is there and watching out for them. One specific package I opened had a flyer for Restored Hope Ministries in it. I wondered how it got there, if on my way from school if I had stuffed it in one of the bags. I remember thinking I should take it out, but I just never did. Then, I thought it was just my laziness, but God never wastes anything. I left the flyer there and continued to make the packages, praying for God to somehow provide me with Bibles because I could not do it on my own.

Bibles are very expensive and there was no way I had the money to buy them for all of my packages. I knew I was supposed to have them in the packages, though. I began to call out to God and ask Him, why He would place such an idea in my head to have Bibles in these packages and not allow me to have the resources? Then, I realized that I forgot how big my God is. This seems silly, but I do it more than I should. I forget that the God I serve created everything. He spoke the Earth into existence. He created everything, why should I doubt that He has the power to allow me to have Bibles in my Grace Packages.

The next day, a friend of mine came up to me and told me that my teacher told her I was looking for Bibles. I told her yes, I really need Bibles, but I have nowhere near the funds to get the Bibles for my care packages. She then told me that she had just come from our church and she needed nine Bibles for a Bible study she had. When she went to the church, they had 240 Bibles there and they didn't have anything to do with them. So, they gave all of the Bibles to her.

Tears started to flow from my eyes, as she continued to tell me that she had 231 Bibles for me waiting in the back of her car that I could use in my Grace Packages. My packages were then complete. Each package would have the ability to meet the physical need and the spiritual need of everyone who was given a package. I just cried in awe of the God we serve. How great is our God? He is Almighty and magnificent. He is all-powerful and all-knowing. He already knew that He placed a burden on my heart for helping in some way with the spiritual need of the homeless population. God allowed me to know how I could not accomplish this task on my own, and even more so, work behind the scenes of my life to make everything work out for the good in the end. God is so great and I was so thankful to be given the Bibles and for everything to fall into place to pass out the Grace Packages in Dallas.

The day came to go to Dallas and to pass out the Grace Packages. I had amazing volunteers with me and we were on fire to help the homeless community. As we were getting into the car to head to Dallas, it was a beautiful sight to see how God could provide. He delivered in seeing all of the Grace Packages in the back of the car packed full.

Then, one of the girl volunteers turned to me and asked me, "Jillian, what exactly do we do? How do we give them the package? How do we know who is homeless?" This question took me by surprise because we all knew the goal was to pass out the packages, but the method was not made clear. A smile formed on my face as God reminded me of how I did not even know if Jane was homeless or not, but God led me to her. Through the simple boxed lunch, God opened the conversation for Jane to come to Christ. As I opened my mouth, I knew amazing things were going to happen that day, "You will give packages to whomever God leads you to. God has already gone before us and prepared the hearts of those who will receive each package. Go up to them and tell them that these packages were made to bless them and just ask them how they are. Ask them their names, just get to know them, and have that listening ear for their prayer requests. God will do the rest." We all got out of the car and prayed for our journey and for God's will to be done.

Those words, for God's will to be done, I heard them all the time growing up in church. They seem so simple and so accurate. The challenge in them is to appreciate and see God in everything He does and to remember God's will may not be our will. For the trip to Dallas, I prayed for someone to be saved, but I also did not know God's will.

As we arrived, there was no one around. The streets seemed to be empty. As we all got out of the car, I prayed again for the Lord to guide us and for His will to be done. Then I split us into groups and we all carried as many grace packages as we could and went on our separate routes. As I went with another volunteer, it seemed like people just came into our path. We were able to pray for a lady right off the bat. It was great to see people so thankful and saying how much of a blessing these packages were. We were out until we had passed out all the packages that we brought with us. When we walked back to the car, we still had a few more packages. Everyone was so eager to share what the Lord had done so far while passing out packages.

My mom thought of the great idea to keep driving a bit and find a new location to see if there were more people that may need the packages. We all got back into the car and were ready to start handing out more packages. Just to see the joy on people's faces made it all worth it. As we were driving, we saw a very frail little old lady and she seemed to be carrying a lot. My mom pulled over and asked her if we could drive her to her destination. She told us that she was trying to get to a store up the street a little ways.

My mom let this little old lady into the car. She was so small. You could practically see right through her, she was all skin and bones, and my heart started to hurt. My mom started to talk to this woman as she gave my mom directions. My mom offered her a package and she proceeded to tell my mom 'no'. The little lady explained how it was way too heavy for her to be carrying around with her and that she did not want it. My mom sweetly asked if she just wanted to take the Bible. The little old lady barked back, "Oh no! I don't want that at all!" My mom just smiled and said, "How about you take everything you want and we will keep the rest?" She agreed to this and started to take a few things out of the grace package. She proceeded to tell us that she was in her sixties and had been on the streets longer than I had even been alive. This broke my heart. I wanted her to take the whole package. I wanted to do so much more for her.

My mom just talked with her, and as I watched my mom talk to this little old lady, I realized all she really wanted was for someone to talk to. Someone to look her in the eyes and treat her like she was equal to them, like she was human just like us. As my mom continued to talk and arrive at her destination, she decided that she would take the Bible. She told us it was a real nice thing that we are doing here. Before she got out of the car and grabbed the Bible, she said something I will never forget, "I need hope more than I need bread." This woman that had been homeless longer than I have even been alive told us that she would rather have hope over anything else.

That moment I have treasured ever since. This is why getting the 231 Bibles was such a miracle. All of the donations and money coming in right when I needed it was such a blessing. All of it fell into place, for such a time as this. In the book of Esther, it talks about her following God's will. "For if you keep silent at this time, relief and deliverance will rise for the Jews from another place, but you and your father's house will perish. And who knows whether you have not come to the kingdom for such a time as this" (Esther 4:14 ESV). Esther was faced with telling the King that she was a Jew, and the

36

order to kill the Jews would be an order to kill her as well. Her cousin urged her to see that just maybe the Lord had placed her in a position so close to the King for such a time as this. I believe this verse fully. Just like Esther, I believed God placed Jane and I together for me to see the overwhelming need of women on the streets. I knew, without a shadow of a doubt, that God placed grace packages on my heart so that I would be able to hear how God's hope is all people truly need. God continues to overflow my cup and allow me to see His countless blessings. My prayer is to follow God and His will, and along the path I am reminded of just how miraculous He truly is. I needed to hear those words from the little old lady. Looking back at the original problem I faced, it seemed impossible to help the entire homeless community. Now, I know I don't need to provide them with everything on their list. I need to show them the hope they have in Jesus Christ. I need to look at them in their eyes and listen to them, allow them to know that I care about them, learn their names, and make them realize that they are so loved.

When it comes down to it, that's all we really want in this world. We all have a deep desire to be loved, to be respected, and to acknowledge that we truly have a purpose. Talking with her that day, we showed her Christ's love and gave her the hope of Christ that fulfills all of those needs. Jesus is the answer to so many of the problems in our lives, if we just listen.

After that conversation, we were all pumped to pass out the final few packages. We saw a huge bulletin board and under it were so many people who were camping out there. My mom parked the car and we got out carrying packages. I went over to a lady in a wheelchair and at first, she was so scared of me. I told her not to be afraid because I just wanted to give her this bag with stuff in it. She started to smile and told me thank you. We all started to talk to various people, but I stayed talking to this lady. I asked her if she was okay, and that was a key question. She started to tell me all about her life. One thing I kept noticing was that her hair was everywhere, all over her face, and she kept blowing it out of the way. Out of the package, I took a comb and asked if I could do her hair as she talked. She put her arm out in front of her and told me, "Honey... you can't, I am too dirty." This broke my heart. I went right in front of her and leaned down so I could be eye level with her. I told her, "I don't care. I want to bless you. Let me do your hair. I love you so much and you can never be too dirty." As I said this, she started crying. She told me how people wouldn't talk to her or even look her in the eye. As I started to brush through her hair, she told me she couldn't remember the last time someone had touched her. I just listened to her and then she stopped talking and asked me, "Why do you love me?" I went back around and told her I love you because you are worth it. I love you because Jesus loves you. He loves you unconditionally. You can never be too dirty or too far away from God for Him not to be able to save you. He can save you right where you are at, and as a Christian, He has called me to love you unconditionally. She started crying and reached out for my hand, then pulled back, looking away from my eyes. She didn't say anything. I just reached out to her and held her hand and told her, "Jesus loves you and He will always love you." She told me thank you for everything and then we had to leave.

I still think of her a lot because so many times we feel like we are too dirty. Not physically, but we are too dirty spiritually or we have done too much. We feel like we have to clean ourselves up again before we come to Christ. But Christ is ready for us at any time. He knows everything that we have done and loves us despite it all. Nothing we can do can mess that up. After that day, I thought how beautiful it is to know that in the midst of all the mess in life that we go through, He still loves us. He still chooses us as His sons and daughters. He still wants us to profess His name and tell others about how His unconditional love washed us clean. I find that so beautiful and appreciated it so much more after passing out the Grace Packages.

Looking back at the project the next day, I was so thankful for all of the amazing conversations we all had and the people we were able to pray for and bless. A part of me was a little disappointed that we were not able to help anyone accept Christ into their lives. I was so grateful for all God had done, but I wondered why. Why didn't anyone accept Jesus?

Chapter Five: Grace Packages

Chapter Six

Conversion

The passion inside me to share the gospel never subsided. If anything, it grew. I would make it a point to bring up Christ into conversations. I wanted to lead not only by example, but also in speech. This process is far from perfect, but I knew with my whole heart that I wanted to serve the Lord.

In the summer of 2015, I was able to go with my church choir again on a mission trip. This mission trip would be out of the country to England! My heart was jumping out of my chest. I get to go to England on a mission trip. The preparation for the trip was absolutely incredible. We had cultural classes, Bible studies, and prayer meetings for our trip. The closer we got to the trip, the more excited I was.

One night, I had the list of pastors, churches, and organizations in front of me that I was supposed to pray for. I started praying for them. Then, I found myself crying out to God. Begging Him to show Himself to me. Begging for a life change. After the prayer, I realized that I wanted God to prove Himself, not in a testing way, but in reassurance. Either way, I felt ashamed after I let the words come out of my mouth, but my heart remained the same. I wanted the Lord to show Himself to me in a mighty way. I prayed that I would be able to stand on my foundation of His name boldly and not be able to be shaken.

On the days preparing for the trip, I started to examine my heart. Why would I want the Lord to prove Himself to me? I believe in Him. I believe in Jesus Christ. Why do I need proof? Then, a small part of my heart ached and I knew the answer. I knew that beyond anything else that I believe in Jesus. The small ache in my heart also knew that I was still in search for an answer to the famous question of: Why do bad things happen?

I felt like I had travelled mountains since I last allowed my heart to ask this question. Since then, I have worked through forgiveness of the person and allowing myself to know that I am not guilty. Through various years, I held my head high and knew that the shame was not mine and the hurt is working for good. Despite all of it, a little part of my heart was revealed that I still wanted God to show Himself. Comfort me again. Protect me again. I wanted to feel His presence again. I allowed that little part of me to wonder about the Lord revealing Himself to me once again as I still prayed for the mission trip in front of me.

The days seemed to fly by as we prepared to go to England. Then, all at once, I was at the airport reporting to go to England. My heart was beating faster than ever before. My excitement level was unconcealable. I wanted to get to England, and I wanted to share the gospel with as many people as possible.

Our large choir was separated into smaller groups to travel and to serve in England. The group that I was placed in was very musically inclined. Many of the soloists were in my group and I began to wonder what our service project would be. When the leaders came to us, they told us that our small group would actually have one more divide. Half of the group would be leading sports camps at the school that we would be serving at. The other half would teach music classes inside, then join the group after school hours to lead an after-school sports camp.

A smile formed on my face hearing the word, "school". For so long, my mission field had been my hallways. I knew for my time as a student that my mission field was the hallways I walked down, the people I passed every day. I loved how the Lord would tie that in even as I travelled outside the country. My own thoughts began to race about how the sports camp would be run and how I would be able to get to know each of my players on my team.

Then, bursting my thought process, my name was called. Coming out of my thoughts, I responded, "Yes?" My leaders were looking at me and told me again, "Jillian, you will be leading the music classes inside the school." My smile fainted a little as I went with the other group members. My immediate response was to laugh. How was I in the group that would teach music? I was in the group with the soloist and I was a dancer. I loved worshipping and singing in the choir as a whole, but I knew better than to think I was a soloist myself. I was so confused as to why I would be in this group.

My mind began to race while we were on the plane headed to England. I wanted to talk to my leaders and explain to them that I didn't believe I was equipped to teach a music class. Then, something tugged on my heart not to. I am on a mission trip and have been praying for the Lord to use this trip to do amazing things for His name. We have prayed over every aspect of this trip and who am I to believe that the Lord made a mistake with this? Who am I to deny that the Lord is the Almighty God and has a purpose beyond what I can see? I knew I needed to check my heart and pray that the Lord would use me even in a place where I did not feel most confident.

Leaving the plane, my passion was pouring out. I could not help but to talk to everyone. I wanted to ask everyone so many questions. I wanted to learn about their lives. I wanted to share with them about mine. I wanted to make an impact in Christ's name. My heart was overjoyed and I knew that Christ had His divine hand within this.

The morning of the first day of teaching music classes, I was nervous. I opened my Bible to do my devotion to see what the Lord would say to me. I smiled at how He knew exactly what was on my heart. That morning I read from Hebrews 13:20-21, "Now may the God of peace who brought again from the dead our Lord Jesus, the great shepherd of the sheep, by the blood of the eternal covenant, equip you with everything good that you may do his will, working in us that which is pleasing in his sight, through Jesus Christ, to whom be glory forever and ever. Amen." My God is so great. God knew I would still feel inadequate to lead these classes, but I wanted to follow His will. Reading this, He reminded me that He doesn't call the equipped, He equips the called. I don't have to be worthy or the best, but my willingness to serve in any aspect He leads me is more than enough. All the worry faded and all I could feel was excitement to see the Lord move in a miraculous way. I had no doubt in my mind that He could.

When we arrived at the school, we received the first class of students. The first class had a pretty large group of girls and they were all dancers! When I saw this, I began to laugh. I was the only dancer in the group. God did come before and knew that I needed to be there. He knew my exact purpose before it was even revealed to me. In the classes, we taught them songs from our concerts and I taught the simple dances to go with them. It was so much fun!

We were able to talk to the students about Jesus through the gospel songs and watch them laugh and perform to the songs they already knew. It was amazing sitting back and watching the joy they found in dancing to these songs and answering the questions they had about the words of the gospel songs. Every minute of teaching the classes was special. The students were so willing to learn and so loving. I was beyond blessed to be there and witness it.

After our day of teaching various music classes, we went out to help with sports camp. I sat at the table signing people in. One girl came up and said she didn't want to be there. Her friend was forcing her to come. She looked at her friend and said she would wait for her, and that she did not play sports. She didn't like sports. She rushed over the wire fence away from the sign-in table.

My heart immediately went out to her. I knew that it could hurt to feel like you are not able to participate in something. Her feelings with sports were my exact feelings that I had on the plane about teaching a music class. I looked over to one of the girls in my group and asked if she could continue to sign people in. She was more than willing to take my place at the table. Once she did, I immediately headed over to the girl sitting by the fence.

As I walked up to her, I realized yet again that the Holy Spirit had prompted me to do something, but I had no clue what I would say. Looking at her, I smiled and sat next to her silently. I tried to rush my mind of things to say, but couldn't think of anything. Finally, I gave up on trying to force something. I just sat next to her in silence. Both of us were sitting there watching the teams form and the other students begin to play sports. Silently, pulling at the grass, she spoke first.

"Why did you come over here?" she asked me. I laughed a little at the question because I was wondering the same thing of myself. I responded back to her, "I didn't want to play sports either." My answer seemed to open a door. She turned to me and started to talk to me. She asked me about my family and where I was from. I told her everything she wanted to know. When I told her I lived in Texas, she asked me if I had a horse and it made me smile. I told her no, but that it would be really cool to have one. The simple questions we asked seemed to slowly flourish a friendship. When the first day of the sports camp ended, she got up and went to walk away with her friend. She turned back to look at me and asked, "Will I see you tomorrow?" and I responded with a huge smile. "Yes, I will see you tomorrow."

Going back that night, I began to pray for her. I prayed for her and her family. I prayed that the Lord would grow our friendship so that I would be able to share Christ with her. I began to pray for the Holy Spirit to give me the words to say.

The next day, we led multiple music classes again. At our break between classes, there was something called tea time. We would have tea and toast in the teacher's workroom. One of my leaders came up to me and asked me about my conversation with the girl yesterday. I told her that we became friends and that I learned the basics about her and her family. We were just forming a relationship. I didn't bring up Christ yet, except to say that we were on a mission trip. My leader asked me if she could pray for me and the girl, and I told her yes. My leader began to pray for our friendship and that the Lord would use it for His divine purpose.

When we went back to teaching classes, there she was. She was in my music class. She walked straight up to me and we started talking like we had been friends for years. Learning the dances and songs, we started laughing and smiling. Then, when we were teaching her and the rest of the class the gospel songs, she stopped and looked at me.

She told me that she assumed that I was a Christian, but she was not. I asked her what religion she was. She told me that she was Muslim and had been brought up in a strict Muslim home all of her life. She began to tell me all about her religion. I sat and listened to her. By the time she finished telling me about her religion, the music class was over and she had to leave to get to her next class. Before she left, she turned again and asked me if we were still friends. I told her of course we were still friends.

As she left, I prayed. I prayed so hard. I asked my group to pray for her. I prayed for me to be able to share my faith with her. I prayed that the Lord would use me as a vessel to show her who Jesus Christ was. I prayed that she would get to at least learn about Jesus. I did not pray for her to become a

Christian. Still to this day, I am disappointed in myself. I prayed many times for God's will to be done, but I did not pray for her to become a Christian. Some part of me must have doubted that it was possible for her to convert in such a short period of time. I am ashamed of my doubt of the power of Christ. But I continued to pray for God's will. I just prayed for a seed to be planted in her heart. I would probably never see that seed of her learning about Christ, fully flourish into a relationship with Him, but that one day it might happen.

After all the music classes that day, she was waiting for me by the fence. We began to talk about her family again. She then asked me about my faith. I openly shared with her about how God saved me. How I felt such a void in my life before He came in. How He made me complete. Jesus came and saved me from all of my hurt and pain in my past and was able to turn my life around. She told me she had never heard anything like that before. She never heard of a full life change. She told me to tell her more about my God. I told her I would love to.

I began explaining to her the story of Jesus. As I was telling her about Jesus, she told me that this was not what she learned her whole life. I asked her what she thought about it. She seemed to chew through all the information she was given. She looked at me and asked if I thought it was okay if we talked about something else. I told her it was definitely okay. We started to talk about what I was going to do with my last year of high school coming up and the rest of my life. I asked her the same, and we began to talk like old friends again.

Chapter Six: Conversion

When the sports camp ended, she didn't ask me if I would see her tomorrow. It was known. The next day of our church group at the sports camp would be the last day and we would want to say goodbye. We went our separate ways. I couldn't help but allow my heart to hurt a little. I was so excited to tell her my testimony; all that God had done in my life. I was so ready to explain to her the story of salvation and all that Jesus Christ has done for me. I was so prepared for her to have some reaction. But there was nothing. I began to pray to the Lord for His will to be done, but to work in her heart.

As the day progressed, it began to sink in that tomorrow was the last definite day that I would be able to see her. Then, I decided to pray boldly. I didn't care about the odds; my whole life was about defying the odds. I began to pray that she would become a Christian and I would get to see it happen. I prayed that something would make her question her religion. Something would shake her worldview. Something would make her want to come to Christ. I prayed for a long time and asked my group to pray for her as well.

That night, trying to go to sleep was close to impossible. It was like I was a little kid about to wake up on Christmas. I knew something was going to happen. I knew that the Lord would move in some way. All doubt was washed from my mind. I knew that my God is great and He is capable of doing anything. Proverbs 21:1 came to my mind. "The king's heart is a stream of water in the hand of the Lord, he turns it wherever he will." If the Lord can turn the king's heart, then He can surely turn her heart. I fell asleep praying for her that night.

In the morning, I popped up out of bed with more energy than ever before. There is something about the power of prayer that when you pray for such a long time, you know the Lord will move in a great way. Your outlook on life is just expecting greatness. All throughout the day, I was pumped to see her and see how the Lord moved.

Finally, all of the music classes were done and I rushed over to the fence to meet her. She wasn't there. Some of the students were already out there, but she wasn't. I patiently waited by the fence as the sports camp began. She still wasn't there. My mind began to race. Did I say something to offend her? Did she never want to see me again? Then, I saw her friend that she showed up with on the very first day. I got up and walked over to her. I asked her friend where she was. She told me that she hadn't seen her today.

My heart sank. All my prayers for something to happen and I would never get to see her again. All the prayers for her and I would never get to talk to her ever again. This realization set in and hurt more than anything. This fact is the hardest fact of mission trips, you become so close to people and you may never see them again.

I went back to the fence, sitting and praying. I still prayed for her even though I knew I would never see her again. I watched the sports camp end and the students starting to walk away. This was my last day and I just prayed that someone would one day tell her about Jesus and it would click in her heart. I prayed, cleaning up the sports camp, that one day something I said may have her question her religion and reach out to someone. In the midst of cleaning up, one of the leaders shouted my name. I looked up and there she was. I ran over to her, and it felt like I hadn't seen her in years. I wanted to tell her how I was so scared I would never see her again and that I possibly offended her. But right when

I walked up, she pulled me close and hugged me. After our hug, she looked me straight in the eyes and said, "Jillian, I want your Jesus." In that moment, I couldn't help it, tears of joy started to rush down my face. I walked her through praying to accept Christ. When we finished she asked me, "Okay, now what do I do to earn your Heaven?" I began telling her how she doesn't have to earn anything. Jesus Christ paid the price. He died for our sins and rose again on the third day. He was the ultimate sacrifice and took our place. All we have to do is accept Him and believe in Him. This made her cry. She told me that all her life she was trying to earn something. I asked her if she fully understood what it meant to be a Christian and she told me yes. She told me everything I told her yesterday. I was amazed that she heard it all. I was astonished that she was now a Christian. She told me how refreshing it was to believe. Then she told me something so profound. She looked at me and said, "Jillian... I get it." I asked her, "What do you get?" She responded back with confidence, "As Christians, we don't have to earn Heaven because Jesus paid the price. All we have to do is accept Jesus. And all we have to do is accept Jesus because once you do, you want to change." Her words made me stop. Her words were so profound. She had only been a Christian for a few minutes but was already teaching me something.

I looked at her and said that is exactly right. Then, she continued to tell me, "I know why you came." I looked at her confused, so she continued on, "I know why you came to England. When you feel this good, you want to share it. Jesus makes you want to be good. Jesus makes you want to tell people about it." All of her words were exactly correct and I knew that she understood. I was so excited to have witnessed her coming to Jesus Christ. My heart was singing like never before and I felt as if I was in a dream.

In the midst of all my excitement, I stopped and asked her, "What made you want Jesus in your heart?" It was in the back of my mind for a little bit, and she laughed a little and answered, "I forgot I didn't tell you. It was the television." I sat there so confused. I told her that I would go and get her a Bible and told the leader of the sports camp that she had accepted Christ into her heart. He got her a Bible and agreed to start discipling her. He said he would love to bring her under his wing and teach her. I was so glad that she was already going to be plugged into a Christian community, so even after this moment, she would still be able to grow and learn about her new faith.

She turned to me so excited to start meeting with the leader of the sports camps and learning more about Christianity. Her eagerness was contagious. Through her, I was reminded of the passion inside me when I first became a Christian and it felt great. I was still puzzled about how a television made her want Jesus. As we were about to leave, I gave her a concert card and invited her to come to one of our concerts before we left England. I told her she could bring her family if she felt comfortable. She told me, "I decided I will tell my older brother about me becoming a Christian and I will ask if only he would like to come." I told her that was great and I hope to see her again. In the back of my mind, I couldn't let it go about the television. So I asked her, "Before you leave, why did the television help you want Jesus?" She looked at me and said, "When I got home, I kept thinking of everything you said. I kept thinking of how your God made you feel so excited, but mine felt like a list of duties. I was thinking about all you said while I was scrolling through the television. I couldn't find anything so I thought I turned it off." I looked at her and said, "You thought you turned a TV off?" She continued to explain, "While I was thinking, I must have hit something on the remote control because it turned on. And when it turned on, it was on a debate with a Christian. As I listened to the Christian, it was like he was answering all my questions. I decided then I want your Jesus. Last night I prayed to have your Jesus." I stood there looking at her completely amazed. It was amazing to hear how the Lord works in people's lives.

As I said my goodbyes, we exchanged social media so that we would still be able to keep in contact. I told her I would miss her so much and if she had any questions to please message me. She left with the biggest smile on her face and she seemed to be glowing. Watching her leave, I was amazed at how much God had done in three days. I told my group of her experience with the Christian debate and how she accepted Christ and they praised the Lord.

I was able to share the story with my whole church choir and it was so great to be able to share how great our God is. How He truly is here. How God really does listen and answer our prayers. Then, in the midst of thinking how great God is, I realized He answered my prayer from before the trip. God allowing me to see her accept Jesus into her heart was Him revealing Himself to me. He was showing me His power, His presence, and His love. He revealed himself to me yet again. I sat in awe of the God I serve. It was like God was sitting right next to me, holding me, telling me to look all around me. He did reveal Himself to me throughout this trip through her, but it was something more than that. It was like the Lord was revealing to me that He is here all along if I choose to open my eyes and see it.

Leaving England, I held on to the memories of the conversations I had with her. She was such an amazing friend in our short time together and such a miracle. I was excited to hear from her again and hear how she was growing in her walk with Christ. In the meantime, it was like God had challenged me as well. I begged and pleaded with Him to reveal Himself to me. He did. It was like He was now challenging me back and telling me, "Now that I have proven myself to you, find me."

The words resonated in my heart. Find Him. In England, God's presence and His answered prayers were so overwhelmingly obvious. What are the odds that she would hit the remote to turn on a Christian debate that would answer all of her questions? What are the odds that in all of England that we would meet? All of this made me smile. I knew I understood exactly what God wanted me to do. He wanted me to find Him in the obvious situations, but also in the situations that may seem impossible. God challenged me to find His presence in every circumstance.

Chapter Seven

Finding Him

When I went back to school, I continued to intern at Restored Hope Ministries. I was super excited to come back in my senior year and to meet some of the new women. I had a new perspective of the power of Christ in my life. I knew that there was power behind each prayer without a doubt. I began to pray for the women at Restored Hope and the new women I would meet.

On the first day back, I went around meeting the new women. All of a sudden, one of the ladies told me I looked so familiar to her. I asked her if she lived near me and we tried to figure out how we knew each other, but nothing connected. We moved past the conversation, concluding it might just be because I have a familiar face. I started to talk with more of the women and got back into the routine of things. Every time I went, I continued to sit in on Bible studies with the ladies just to get to know them.

One day, in a Bible study session, we were sitting there and all of the women had to explain why they were there and what led them to come to Restored Hope Ministries. For some women, their parents, family members, or friends

55

found the safe house and they agreed to come. Others just said that they hit rock bottom and went to a local church that pointed them to Restored Hope Ministries. In all of the situations, Restored Hope Ministries was exactly what the women needed and there was a path that the Lord allowed them to take to get to the safe house.

Then, the lady that said she thought she knew me went. She said that she found herself homeless again. She didn't have anything. She didn't know what to do. She told us she was walking on a corner and these two teenagers walked up to her and handed her some green bag with all of these groceries in it, a Bible, and a flyer for Restore Hope Ministries. Her story made me pause. Then, it was like everything connected. Immediately, I started crying in the meeting. All of the women rushed over to me and were making sure I was okay. I looked at her and I told her, "I do know you. That was me."

She came over to me and wrapped her arms around me and held me close. We held each other and just cried. It is amazing how the Lord can work such great miracles. He uses everything for good. She continued to tell the group, with tears staining her face, that she made a bargain with God right before we walked up that if He got her off the streets, she would follow Him. She needed help. She needed some basics to take care of herself and she would start to clean herself up. Then, we walked up with everything she needed and a flyer to the safe house that is now helping to change her life.

I still am amazed at how Christ works everything for good. I remember being a little disappointed that I didn't get to see how He was working that day, when again, He was working everything for the greater good. God knew what she needed. God knew that we were going to be there in that location with everything she needed. This does not happen by coincidence. If my group came one day earlier or later, or if we would have been one block over, we would have never crossed paths. God just knew exactly what she needed and what time she needed it. God is so great and I couldn't hold in my joy.

As she continued to tell her testimony of how she got to Restored Hope, I sat amazed in the presence of the Lord. I thought of Romans 8:28, how it says, "And we know that for those who love God all things work together for good, for those who are called according to his purpose." This verse reminded me that even though I couldn't see how God was working in that moment with my Grace Packages, He was. We prayed for God to go before us and He did. I desperately wanted someone's life to change because of the blessing of grace packages and her life did. It was amazing how God allowed me to see His hand almost half a year later. He allowed me to see that He was working for His divine goal all along. I was placed there for a reason and it was like He was letting me in on the secret, revealing to me a part of His greater plan. He provided her a pathway to Restored Hope Ministries.

Now, through Restored Hope Ministries, she graduated from the program and is doing so well, all because the Lord has a plan for our lives and knows how to work everything for good. I am so thankful that I was able to be used as a vessel in His plan. I love how we can't see all that the Lord has in store for us, but He will always work it out for good.

So many times, in church and in life, we hear the great saying that it will all work out for good. Everything? Everything will work out for good. I always was a little skeptical of that after the nightmare I went through for three years and after seeing all of those colorful hands on the wall that experienced the same kind of hurt. I didn't know how Christ could possibly use that for good. But after walking with Christ, He has revealed little reasons to me. He has offered me to see His presence in mighty ways and in ways only I could see. He was training me to find Him.

I decided that I would continue to try to find Christ in every situation. This gave me a new mindset as I returned to Restored Hope Ministries. I would find Christ in everything and help the women to find Him as well. After interning at Restored Hope Ministries for a while, many of the women were very comfortable and could talk to me about a lot. One lady was more shielded off than everyone else. I could tell her pain was immeasurable and I didn't know what happened, but I prayed that God would give me the opportunity to talk with her.

Coming in one day, the women were in the middle of a Bible study about forgiveness. They were having to write who had wronged them in their lives and if they had fully forgiven them. This task hit really hard for me because I did not know if I had even fully forgiven the person who hurt me. He seemed to take what seemed like everything from me. I was thinking of this while walking around the group and talking with the women. I didn't know if I should even sit in with this study because I didn't know if I was qualified.

Now, I know those thoughts that were having me doubt myself were coming from Satan. God does not call the equipped, He equips the called. Even though I am not perfect and will never be, I needed to be there to support the women through this difficult task. I noticed that the lady that was a little more shielded was staring at her paper. I went over to her and started to talk with her. I asked her if she thought the assignment was difficult and when she looked up at me, I could see she was trying to hold back the tears. I looked at her and asked if she wanted to talk about it. I asked her who hurt her. She never told me who, but she told me that they had molested her when she was a child. She told me how she lost all of her worth that night. She continued on to tell me how she thought her body didn't matter anymore and that's why she turned to the streets when she got older. I could hear the anger in her voice and see the fire that was burning inside of her. I knew that the same fire in me was burning in her at that moment. She looked at me and told me that he changed her whole life; he ruined it for her.

Chills went up and down my spine. I had spent so many years running from what happened to me. Not facing it and not forgiving. So many people wanted to try to tell me what would help when they didn't even know the toll of what I went through. I spent so much of my life just determined to defy every statistic faced in front of me, trying to deny the label that was placed on me all of those years ago. As I sat there, I was looking into her eyes and I knew she felt the fire I did when I was faced with that wall of colorful hands. I knew she understood the anger that filled me when they labeled me as a victim.

I looked at her and told her that I was so sorry. I told her that I knew she probably heard those words a lot from people that have never experienced, and will never experience, anything like she had gone through. I told her that there was a pain that was eating away at her soul and she has finally let it out. I began to tell her what happened to me, not to relate or to make her feel bad for me. Still to this day, I don't know why I told her, other than God placed me there to tell her. I told her everything I have ever felt. I told her the disgust and shame I felt with myself and all the statistics they told me. It seemed like we were talking for hours. Finally, she emptied herself. When she began, she started off so angry, and then she began to cry and I could tell that this whole time she was trying to stay strong. She was trying to hold it all together because she never wanted to be viewed as weak as she felt in that moment ever again.

Then she asked me how I dealt with everything that happened to me. I was honest with her and told her that there was no way I could have gotten through any of it without Jesus on my side. I told her I still get angry and upset sometimes. I still wake up in the middle of the night sweating and screaming because I was dreaming about it again. I told her she has to start with knowing that it was not her fault. Then, she needs to move onto knowing that Jesus loves her. This made her start to cry and she hugged me and we looked at each other, silent for a long time. We both knew that we went through something that hurt so much. We bonded so much in that moment, but when she finally broke the silence, it seemed like she stripped my whole world.

She broke the thick silence with the question that we all ask ourselves when awful things happen in our lives, "Why?" At this question, a huge lump formed in my throat because I had asked that question so many times. I knew I couldn't have gotten through the awful nightmare without Christ in my corner. I knew that I was falling apart for a long time until I started the process of healing. I looked back and thought of everything that had happened in my life. The big question, why? In this case, the life shattering question, why?

My lips started to form the words 'I don't know' because inwardly, I still don't know why, but what came out of my lips that day was, "This is why." She nodded like she understood and began to work on the process of starting to forgive the person that stole her life from her. As I sat there, I knew the Lord had given me the words, but I pondered over their meaning.

"This is why." That simple phrase held so much weight. I never really saw it until then. I was surrounded by women that became the statistics I tried so hard to defy, but only by the grace of God did I make it and did I defy those statistics. I was surrounded with women who have experienced a hurt that many of us will never even grasp the concept of. I was surrounded by women that came off the streets, the women just two years earlier Christ called me to serve.

I felt a warmth rush over my body when I realized, again, this is why. These women, right here, are the reason why I had to go through all of that pain. These women needed guidance and someone to understand what they have gone through. These were women who struggle with feeling too far from Christ because of what they have done or what has been done to them. These women had their lives taken from them and are on the journey to getting it back. I realized looking at each of their faces that they are the reason.

As I drove home, it was like I had the ultimate epiphany moment. The rest of my anger left me that day as I realized that it was all a part of God's plan. It seems cliché and cheesy, but God does even use the worst of things for good. I don't ever think I will say it was worth it. I can say confidently that out of something that was no good and completely corrupt, God pulled beauty. In the midst of my nightmare, God created a purpose. I can speak to women who are hurting and empathize with them on a level that I would not have been able to if I wasn't put through that trial. Now, I am able to be used for God's greater purpose, all because of a trial I had to face alone. Because of it, I can help other women through it. I finally found Christ in the midst of my nightmare.

Chapter Eight

Accidents Have Purpose

The morning of September 24, 2015, I was driving back from my concurrent classes at the local community college. As a 17-year-old girl, I was behind the wheel of my yellow Volkswagen Beetle. I was driving and just had to go straight ahead about a quarter of a mile back to my high school for classes. The two lanes suddenly merged into one and the other car did not see how fast it was coming. I can only assume the woman saw a rush of orange cones closing her lane and my rush of yellow to get into the other lane. Well, her choice was to slam right into my car. She hit me and created my very first car accident.

Many can remember their very first car accident, and I will never forget mine. I immediately called my mom. The phone went to voicemail. It was like a rush of everything I have ever learned was spinning around in the car whispering for me to do it, but I couldn't. I couldn't just do anything. I tried to pull over to let other cars pass, but my head started hurting. Then, one of the whispers finally set in to my mind. Call 911.

Chapter Eight: Accidents Have Purpose

I called the police and remember trying to tell them where I was. The tears started to roar from my face. I could barely speak. Then, like a flash, the police were there. They had the woman out of her car talking to them and the two police officers kept looking at me. I was sitting there frozen. I was mortified as to what had just happened, but even more blessed looking over my body that everything was fine.

This reminded me of a story, later on, that my mom told me: "When you were a baby girl... I was so blessed and so overjoyed to see you. I took you into my arms, and I started counting your ten little toes and ten little fingers. I wanted to make sure you were all healthy. You were. And I cried of joy." In that moment, I checked myself to see everything was in place. I was not hurt externally and I just started crying. At this point, the police officers may have guessed that I was younger because one of the officers came over and asked me to open my door and I did. He looked at me and immediately I knew I was safe. This police officer walked me through the entire process. He asked me for my phone to take pictures of the other car. He took pictures of my car. He asked where I kept my insurance ... he took care of everything.

Then, the police officer came back to me and asked me how I was feeling and if I remembered what happened. With streaks of tears, now dried, burning onto my face I croaked that, "I think I am fine. I feel fine. I just want my mommy. All I remembered was getting slammed into and my side hitting the middle console." He continued to take care of everything and gave me my phone when he saw my mom calling. I talked to my mom and she was now on her way to meet me at the school. The police officer looked at me and told me, "I know this is a scary time right now, but you will be okay. Do you believe that?" I just nodded my head right back at him. Realizing only then that there was something completely different about him.

I was escorted back to my high school to wait for my mom to pick me up. The police officer took care of everything, calling the police officer at my school, letting her know that I was in a car accident and will not be attending school today. I was checked out of school as soon as my mom arrived.

When my mom appeared, it was like a whirlwind of emotions hit me. She was crying as I could see in her eyes and her hands were touching me making sure that I was okay. I was alright. She cried and held me and asked me how I felt. I just remember saying I was fine but just wanted to go home. As I got in the car, I told my mom about the police officer and how he took care of everything for me. How I didn't have to lift a hand or anything. My mom looked at me and told me how she is so glad that God sent someone to be there for me to protect me and guide me. I remember pondering on this.

Everything came in like a rush when I was in the Emergency Room. They did scan after scan. In one, I believe it was the CAT scan, a nurse told me that she was sorry for all of the scans and tests they are doing on me, but they just wanted to make sure I was completely healthy. I nodded at her as I tried to show her I understood. She told me that in this scan I will not be able to move for a long time so we can talk if I want. I never remember talking to her. I just remember mentally chewing everything that had just happened. After my wreck, my first call was my mom, who could not be there. But there was this police officer that took care of everything for me. Absolutely everything. I couldn't help but wonder if he was God sent. If this was Christ's touch in the situation. There can always be good found in every situation and as a Christian we do not see how the rest of the world sees. In Matthew 13:16-17 it says "But blessed are your eyes, for they see, and your ears, for they hear. For truly, I say to you, many prophets and righteous people longed to see what you see, and did not see it, and to hear what you hear, and did not hear it." This verse pinpoints how, as Christians, we don't see the world the same. People long to see what we see. We should be able to find Jesus in every situation and because of that, we can see the good in every situation. People long to see the good in everything, but they do not see as we see.

If you have ever worn glasses, you have had this experience on your own. You go throughout your life doing your own thing for such a long time. Then, one day the optometrist tells you that you will be needing glasses. Everything that needs to go into getting a person glasses happens, but then there is the moment when your glasses come in.

When I was little, I remember putting on my glasses and not understanding that I needed them, until I had them on. Once I placed the glasses on, it all became clear, literally. I did not know how much I was missing until I placed the glasses on.

Chapter Eight: Accidents Have Purpose

I remember taking off my glasses and putting them back on multiple times. I would have never known what I was missing. And it was something completely beautiful.

It is the same thing with having spiritual eyes. We do not know how much we are missing until we recognize that all God does is for our good. Then, we can truly place on the spiritual glasses to see out into our lives. Our spiritual glasses will help us see the world as a better place. We will be able to pinpoint light when everyone else can only see darkness. We will be able to find the one flower in the soil that seems barren. We will see the crack of sunlight trying to fight off the darkness. In everything, we will see things through the eyes of having our Eternal Father, who loves us with an unconditional love. Sometimes, people never see the difference until they place on their glasses.

I realized through all of my encounters that morning that I needed to focus on the good. The good placed in front of me, was the police officer. He was my strength, protection, and helper. He was Christ's touch in the whole situation. One person and one good thing can change a whole situation. Then all of a sudden, I had to leave the machine behind and was placed into a room for the doctor to come and talk to my family and me.

Little did I know that the moment between my Savior and me in all of the scans was much needed. All that was in the past was just battle one. The funny thing is, in Christ we already have the victory, but in our life situations we often forget that. With battle one over, I was ready to hear from the doctor and go home. One thing I have learned is you are either exiting a battle, about to go into a battle, or in a battle when it comes to life. And many times, we don't even know where we stand.

Chapter Nine

Power in Prayer

I was trying to fall asleep and rest, but because they found out that I had a concussion, no one was letting me rest. No one was even letting me sleep. Waiting for the doctor just seemed like the finale of today's show was finally going to come to an end.

Then, the doctor walked in. There was a solace about him. He did not seem sad, but he did not seem happy. My mind rushed back to when I was a freshman in high school and my medical terminology teacher told us how we should approach patients. The lesson was a very long list of "do's and don'ts," but the main idea of the lesson that I pulled was: do not scare the patients with what you know and do not let them read anything from your face. It will worry them. Looking at this doctor, I felt like we were having the same thought process because his face wasn't happy or sad. Finally, he told us, "I have good news and bad news for you all today. The good news is Ms. Jillian did not obtain any serious injuries. From the wreck, she has a minor concussion, but besides that, she is healthy." I was overjoyed to hear those words. Now, I can go home. Looking back at the doctor I forgot… he had bad news as well. He continued on to say, "We did find a prior existing condition. Jillian…" The doctor seemed to talk in slow motion. Nothing was moving fast enough. I thought I was healthy. Thought? I am healthy. There is nothing wrong with me at all. I am fine. I had to slowly settle down my brain to hear what he was trying to tell me, but I missed it. Everyone's eyes in the room went to me and looked so hurt and worried. I looked into my mom's eyes and it was like she was trying to fend off the tears. I looked back at the doctor, and I think he understood that I had no idea what was going on.

He then said, "You have two tumors, one on each ovary. The one on the right side is the size of a grapefruit and if you lay back, you can feel it yourself. The other on the left, is the size of a lemon." He continued on to talk about how he was not a specialist in this area and could not tell us anymore than that. We would need to talk to a specialist.

Well, I was sitting there and my world froze. Two tumors? Why is everyone still talking and saying things? I have two tumors. What does this mean … I don't understand … All of these thoughts were swirling around in my mind and I was just so tired. I believe now that I was also spiritually tired. I had just left one battle to walk straight into the next, and this is how it is sometimes in life. In 1 Peter 5:6-7 it says, "Humble yourselves, therefore, under the mighty hand of

God so that at the proper time he may exalt you, casting all your anxieties on him, because he cares for you." In this moment, I knew I was too tired to deal with this on my own. Also, I reminded myself of all I have learned, my burden is never meant to be carried on my own. I am called to give my burdens and anxieties to the Lord. I tried to focus on this as my world kept spinning.

My heart sunk into the pit of my stomach. The room seemed to evaporate away. Somehow, in the midst of the chaos of this news, I just started to question everything. "Why was I put on this earth just to possibly have cancer my senior year of high school? What is the point of living if I still believe I have so much more to do?" I thought of the people who were diagnosed with cancer in my life and how kind and sweet they are. I became so angry. I could feel myself fuming from the inside. How? How could these people diagnosed with cancer be so thankful for each day they live knowing that the next one isn't promised? In James 4:13-15 it says, "Come now, you who say, 'Today or tomorrow we will go into such and such a town and spend a year there and trade and make a profit' yet you do not know what tomorrow will bring. What is your life? For you are a mist that appears for a little time and then vanishes. Instead, you ought to say, 'If the Lord wills, we will live and do this or that.'" I knew what the Bible said about each day not being promised. I knew that we are like a mist that vanishes in time, but there is always a difference between hearing it and living it. In this moment, I was living it. I started to look over to my mom, who seemed to be trying to hold it all together. But in the midst of all this support, I felt alone. I was now carrying what seemed to be an immeasurable burden.

The doctor continued to tell us how he was not a specialist. He could not tell me anything about the tumor, my health, or anything regarding it except that it was there. He said that we would have to make an appointment with a specialist, then they would refer us to a surgeon. He wished us best of luck. While walking out I felt as if every eye was on me, waiting for me to crumble. But I was fuming on the inside, the pain and tears had not set in. As we left, my mom looked over to me and told me that tonight would be a good night to go watch the movie *War Room*.

The Christian movie had been in theaters for a little while now and we were hearing all of the great reviews over it, but never had the time. My mom advised me, which was wise counsel, to cling to the Lord in this time and to try not to become upset over what could be when we do not know. This is so true and in the midst of many battles in our life, we need people that will always direct us back to the Lord. Because at the end of the day many people may think they can give sound advice or may think they know how to solve a problem you are in, but nobody knows the future except the Lord. No one knows the plans ahead but God. In this situation, I learned to seek the Lord.

The ride to the movie theater seemed to blur, but I remember the thoughts rushing over me. I kept thinking of my purpose and how I was trying to bargain with God and tell Him that I have so much to offer and not to let me go. I was pleading with the Lord for it not to be my time. The tears slowly started to roll down my cheeks as I knew that I had no control over what was going to happen and what I was going to find out. Everything is in the Lord's hands and I have to be able to trust in Him and allow His plan to work. I knew all of the right things... I was taught all of the right things. But in the situation, none of them felt right. None of them felt near and dear to my heart. They all seemed like factless clichés rolling off the tongues of people who didn't understand.

As we walked into the movie theater, my heart felt like it was callousing over. I did not want to watch a Christian movie and hear how great God is all the time. I wanted a specialist appointment. I wanted to know my health. I wanted to know the future now. I did not know that this movie was going to be one of the main things that helped me through the fear of the unknown.

The movie spoke to the trials in our lives and how we are going through a war in life. Satan is constantly asking God for permission to tempt us and give us trials. Then, the movie focused on the power of prayer, how for Christians, our prayer is our fight and the prayer room was the war room. My huge takeaway from the movie was how we need to fight for everything in our lives. We need to fight through prayer and let God do the rest. In this, we need to understand that prayer is not a passive action to be taken, but is an active fight and stance in our relationship with Christ. God hears each prayer, each plea, each cry out to Him. He knows what we are going through, and even more than that, He knows why we are going through it. So, if we lean upon Him, He will surely lead us out of the storm.

I sat at the end of the movie, in tears. Silent tears. They quietly stretched down my face. I couldn't believe that this movie was the exact encouragement I needed. It convicted me in how I was doubting already my relationship with Christ and how powerful my God was. I knew I needed to step back and ask myself the question. Jillian... How big is your God? The answer I knew, but earlier I was buried beneath anger, fear, and hurt. My God is all-powerful, He is a mighty Savior, He is a provider, protector, healer, and He is the Great I Am. So why would I live in fear? There has never been a moment that has surprised the Lord and I knew now that this was somewhere in His plan.

The first office visit to the specialist finally came. The wonder of everything I would find out was a cloud following me everywhere. I couldn't tell my small group at church or anyone because the thought of saying it out loud just made it a little more real and I did not want any of this nightmare to become real. Walking into the office, the elephant in the room became even more prominent. I walked into the four white walls that seemed to be holding the answer to a question that was holding my life in the balance. The specialist was very kind. She told us that she looked over the scans. She tried to explain all of these medical terms and all of the possibilities of how these two tumors may have formed. At the end of the day, I was just waiting for my clean bill of health.

Then, she addressed me. "Do you want kids?" What kind of question is this, I thought to myself. Out loud I responded, "Yes, I would love to have kids in the future." Then, it hit me, and I couldn't believe it did not hit me before. You need ovaries to have children. The tumors are on both of my ovaries. I do not even have one healthy ovary. She then went on to explain she could not tell us if it was cancer or not, but the tumors needed to be taken out immediately. The one on the right, which was a size of a grapefruit, was so large that if anything could happen to it that it may move, then it could do serious damage. She said it was a blessing that the tumor did not move during my car accident, and it was even more of a blessing that we found the tumors through the car accident, because I would have never even known.

Still, she continued on to tell me how there were various possibilities on how to take out the tumors. She did inform me that I might not be able to keep both of my ovaries, because of the size of the tumors, but she knows the surgeon will try. The pain sunk in more than ever. I might not be able to have kids.

She asked me if I wanted to have kids to see the importance of my ovaries to me. She asked me these questions to form a method to save my ovaries. All of this started to pile into my brain and I realized that I may never get to have a child. I may never get to have the blessing of giving birth to my child and seeing what a wonderful blessing it can be. Immediately, I thought of the Bible story of Sarai and Abram in Genesis 16 of how she had Abram sleep with her female servant because she could not have a child. This story always seemed silly to me. Why would you let your husband sleep with another woman, just to have a child? Then, the Lord pointed out how little her faith was because she took the situation into her own hands instead of waiting for God's divine plan. Then, she was able to have a child, but she created a mess. She made her bed and now she had to lay in it.

I always thought Sarai acted way too prematurely. Like you want to go back in time and ask her, "Why couldn't you just see God's plan? Why couldn't you just be still and know that everything will work out for the glory of Christ?" But how many times do we do this in our own lives? I never thought I would want to prematurely jump before God's plan for my life. I never thought I would try to take my life into my own hands instead of trying to obediently listen to God's will, until this moment in the doctor's office. It all suddenly clicked in my mind. Sarai could not see how it was possible in her own eyes, so she thought she had to take control. In this moment in my life, I was wondering why I hadn't taken control of my life. I was back to my doubt that God had just delivered me from.

I started to contemplate how I could have gone outside of God's plan. I could have gotten pregnant and been a teenage mother, which to the world, may seem awful, but at least I would be able to have a child. At least I would be able to have a son or daughter to call my own. I didn't hear anything else that office visit. All of it went in one ear and out the other. All I could mentally chew on was the possibility of never having kids.

The next day, when I got out of classes, I had to pick up my "nanny children." Waiting in the carpool lane, I just started to bawl and I cried out to God asking Him, "Why? Why would you take this from me? Why would you put the burden of not having children and possibly having cancer on me? I am the person who looks at children and sees the beauty in each smile and laugh. I love children. I want to be a mother, Lord. Please, do not take this from me. Please do not steal this from me. I need to have children. I need to." As I wiped away my tears, the kids got into the car, and I drove to their house. We talked about their day and I helped them with homework, all while still looking at them and wondering if I will ever get to do this with my own children. Will I ever get to see my child want to play on the trampoline instead of doing addition? Or need help coloring in a poster for a project due the next day? Will I even get to live to my high school graduation or will you take me beforehand?

All of these questions started to consume me. The questions not only started to consume me but also started to consume my life. Sadly, I started distancing myself from the Lord. I did not read my Bible every day. In church services, I would sit and listen, but I would not want to learn anything from it. I didn't want to take anything away. I wanted to come and sit and leave the exact same way because that was something I could control in my life, whether I chose to listen or not. I stopped pursuing everything. I did not want to go to club meetings and I did not want to apply to do anything. God blessed me with early acceptance to a lot of schools because if not, I don't believe I would have been able to apply anywhere. I drowned myself into a state of self-loathing. I did not want to be happy and I did not want to see a light at the end of the tunnel. I did not want to smile or laugh. I wanted to know. I wanted this nightmare to be over. I wanted this not to be real, but it was all too real.

One Sunday, my small group leader talked to me. She pointed out that I had been very distant and asked if I had anything on my heart. At this point, I realized that I was letting Satan rule my life. I was allowing my situation to determine my mood and the way I acted, when my character and the way I live for Christ should never ever depend on situations. Situations change like a gust of the wind, but a foundation in Christ is something I can stand firm upon. I allowed myself to do the thing that I was fearing for so long; I allowed myself to make my situation to become more real and tell my small group.

I told them and they all surrounded me as I cried because I knew it was no longer just my battle, but they would be fighting with me as well. My small group and my small group leader began to pray over me, and something happened. Some of the weight of the burden I was carrying was lifted.

I no longer had to fight this fight on my own, but with prayer warriors in my small group by my side.

I realized that it was a ploy of Satan to keep me isolated all along. Isolated, he knew that I would dwell on my thoughts and be lost in my own self-pity. With fellow Christians by my side, Satan knew that I would become strong in the body of Christ because now they are praying with me and alongside me. Now that my struggle was brought into the light, I was able to move forward.

Allowing my small group to know made me realize that I took a step in the right direction, but I was far from being okay. The next day, when I went back into my quiet time after a long time away, the Lord spoke to me. I knew He was asking me, "My child, why are you running? Why are you angry?" This question kept tossing around in my mind. I kept denying it, that I'm no longer running from the Lord. I might have been at first when I just found out. But God, look at me now. I told my table group and they are praying for me. I opened up my Bible today. I am not running and I am not angry. Well, not angry at my God, but angry with the situation. Today, I can spot my denial from a mile away, whereas then, I truly tried to convince myself of this fact.

Later on that week, we had a worship session for my student ministry at my church. I went in with the intention of singing worship songs, all of the feel-good easy Christian things that I thought I could gloss over. The truth was, with the first song the Lord penetrated my heart. I felt a conviction of how fake I was being and the questions again came into my mind. I knew I needed to be honest with myself. I was told over and over in my mind to be truthful. The worship leader and everyone around me started to sing, "You are good, you are good." Finally, my lips sealed shut. My eyes began to water and I knew I could not allow myself to sing that lie. I recognized I was angry with God. The God that saved me. The God who I knew how great and powerful He is. I was angry with Him. I hated myself for being so angry with my Savior. I knew that I was running from God. Deep down in my heart, I thought, just maybe, if I run far enough away from God, He will change His mind. He will change what is in store for me because He knows I am not strong enough to handle it.

I walked away from the worship service towards the back, with every intention of leaving. I ran straight into my girl's minister. She held me close and I just let all my tears out. I didn't know I could have any more left. After I got it all out, I told her that I was worried and I was angry. I didn't want to have cancer. I wanted children more than I have ever wanted anything else. I didn't want this to be the end. I want to graduate. I want to get married one day. I have so many things that I still want to do. And with a lump forming in my throat I asked, "What if I don't get to do any of these things?" I remember she reminded me to look toward Christ. I need to stand on my rock that is Christ Jesus. He knew each day I was going to live even before I was born. He knows the plan. Then, she challenged me and asked me, "Is our Lord good?" At the time, I laughed a little and said of course.

And then she prayed over me. She asked if she could come to the surgery and I told her she could.

Walking away from her, I went over to the wall and sunk to the floor. What kind of question is it ... Is the Lord good? Of course He is good! Why wouldn't God be good? Of course my Savior is powerful. Then, I had a rush all over my body and I remember sitting there in the midst of everyone worshipping and I realized everything she wanted me to see and what Christ was bringing to my heart. Despite the situation, God is good. As a little girl, I remember hearing all of these church folks coming in and saying "God is good" and the next person would respond back, "All the time, He is good." The saying seems so mindless. But it became real to me.

I bowed my head and everything else faded away. I prayed in a way I never had before. I just talked to my Lord, and it was the most bare and raw prayer I have ever had. I just whispered... "Jesus, Jesus, Jesus. Please save me. Please save me from this anger that has consumed me. Lord, I am sorry I doubted your power. I am sorry I would ever try to turn from you. Lord, I dare ask that you let me be healthy and I get to have kids. BUT, God I know... if not, you are still good. Jesus, if I have cancer you are good. If I am healthy, you are good. If I am never able to have kids, you are good. If I am able to have kids, you are good. If none of this is in your plan, you are good. No matter my situation, you are good. And I know that now." When I raised my head from that prayer. ALL of the burden was lifted from me.

Everything was shifted from me carrying the weight of the world onto my powerful Savior carrying the weight for me, and that is exactly how it was intended to be.

When I got up off the ground, the pastor was making an announcement to go and write on a piece of red paper who God is to us. Then, one of the last songs of the night came on. The words stopped me in my tracks. I listened carefully. Everyone sang around me, "You split the sea so I could walk right through it." I knew the analogy was to Moses going across the Red Sea. This analogy became my saying from that point on. The song wasn't only addressing biblical times of how the Lord helped Moses and the Israelites across the Red Sea. The song was also referring to how the Lord will always have a pathway through every trial we may be facing. Even when we can see no way out, our God can do the impossible.

Moses must have been looking at that sea and asking himself how he got there and why the Lord would take them that far just to fail then. With more trouble with the pharaoh and his men on the way, the pressure upon Moses and his faith must have been immense. Moses turned to God. Where Moses and no one else saw a way, God created a way by splitting the Red Sea. God split the sea so they could walk right through it. Realizing all of this, I decided I knew exactly which word I would write onto my card.

I walked right over to the station, picked up a red card and wrote down the boldest word that I believed my God is. I wrote "Healer." At the time, I did not know what my future held, but I knew that God knew. And I believed that He could heal me. I folded the red piece of paper into my wallet and kept it there, to be reminded at any time that I began to doubt God that God was my Healer.

The day of surgery came and my heart was beating out of my chest. I knew that it was in God's hands, but I thought, "Today is the day. Today is the day that will shape my life, which will allow me to see what God has in store for me. I will learn my purpose through this situation." As I walked into a massive hospital, my hand clung to my mother's, holding on tightly.

We got through all of the pre-operational details and they told me I could wait in the waiting room because there was a party waiting for me. When I walked into the room there were many people waiting, possibly for someone to get out of surgery or to go in. Then, I spotted my student ministry's staff. They came over to me and told me how they have been waiting for me and how they have been praying for me. They were all smiling and had such a light coming through them that I felt a hope in the presence of other Christians. This hope was of their prayers and of the faith we all had together that our God can do the impossible. As they started to pray over me, I felt safe. I felt the protective power of my Almighty God rushing over me. In that moment, I did not hold any fear and knew exactly that everything was in His hands. After the prayer, one of the ministers came up to me and gave me a little cross. Inside was a poem. The title of the poem was "A Cross in My Pocket."

The poem shared that this was a cross to carry with me to know that the Lord's presence is with me. I found a peace in it, not in the material of the cross, but of what it represented. The cross represented that even in this immeasurable trial standing before me, the Lord has everything in control and will walk with me through it. Deuteronomy 31:6 came to mind "Be strong and courageous. Do not fear or be in dread of them, for it is the Lord your God who goes with you. He will not leave you or forsake you." I found such a peace with that verse in the back of my mind and rubbing my fingers over this small cross. My youth minister told me that this little elderly lady in the corner made it and was handing it to people before they went into surgery. I went over to her and told her that I was going into surgery today and thank you for reminding me of how great our God is. She told me she would pray for me. That little elderly lady, along with countless prayers, helped lift me up to the Lord before I went into my battle.

Before going into surgery, I felt at peace. I knew that no matter the outcome that the Lord was still good. I reminded myself that my God is so much bigger than my circumstances. I looked over to my mom and she prayed over me a final time. The whole prayer of the innermost part of my heart was still praying for a miracle. I didn't want to speak it out loud because I knew I had full faith in the Lord's plan being greater than my own. I looked over to my mom after the prayer and asked her, "What if they take my ovaries?" Then, she looked at me with her eyes turning glassy like tears were about to fall and she explained to me, "Jilli …

they will have to call out to me before they take out either of your ovaries, but I will let you know the outcome right when you get out of surgery, hunny." That was the final reassurance I needed. It seems silly to find reassurance in the fact they will have to ask my mom before they take out either of my ovaries, but I have faith that my mom knows exactly what to do.

The anesthesiologist gave me anesthesia and I soon was completely knocked out, fully dependent on the Lord.

Before that day, I had never had surgery, ever. When I woke up it felt like I was watching a movie with the dramatic effects of everything being blurred because the character was in a dream. In the midst of the blur, I woke up to see my small group leader bringing in my favorite chocolate shake from Chick-fil-A and my friends and family surrounding me. I couldn't remember much, but realized that they were there and that I was out of surgery. I looked over to my left and my mom was by my side holding and rubbing her thumb over my hand.

I guess I slipped out of consciousness because when I woke back up again there were no people, just my mom and me. I looked over to her and through my lips I croaked, "Like sunlight burning at midnight, making my life something so beautiful, beautiful." Words to a song that we had been listening to on the ride up to surgery. She carefully started to sing with me. She seemed to read my mind as I croaked the words.

She leaned over and whispered in my ears, "I get to be a grandma one day." Tears started to flow from my face as I realized I still was able to have kids. The song "Beautiful, Beautiful" was so true. How in the midst of the darkest of times, God's light can still shine through. I slipped back to sleep.

When I woke up again, I was being admitted to stay overnight. My mom was by my side still. As we were placed in my room for the night, she explained to me the logistics of my surgery. She told me that when they went into my right ovary and tried to remove the tumor, the tumor was too large. This tumor was the size of the grapefruit and there was no way to save my ovary. They called out to my mom and she gave permission that they could take it. She then told me that they went over to my left ovary to take out the tumor the size of a lemon. When they went to take out the tumor, they were faced with a completely healthy ovary. The tumor was gone…

A warmth filled all over my body and all I could say is "God is good." I kept repeating that to myself over and over again that God is good. I was overwhelmed with emotions and could not help but to praise my God. I looked over to my mom as she continued to tell me that I can have children in the future with one ovary. She explained that they do have to biopsy the tumor they did remove and let us know the result at my post-surgery appointment.

My heart was so full ... the Lord took away the tumor. The Lord made the impossible possible. He is such a mighty God. I could never have even prayed or imagined that the tumors or even one of the tumors to just disappear. But He knew His plan, He knew exactly the plan for my life. God is so good. I could not stop praising the Lord and I just laid in my hospital room in awe of the power of my Savior. I have heard and read about miracles, but I never could have ever imagined that the Lord would work one right within me.

I was on cloud nine after my surgery. I knew we did not know the results of the biopsy yet, but there is something about after God performing the impossible once, there are no restrictions on what the Lord can do in my life or anyone else's. We did get the call that the results were in and had to drive up to the surgeon's office.

There was a different feel walking into his office this time. Waiting in the waiting room wasn't an anticipation if God will provide or what God's plans will be. This time waiting, I was positive that God was my Healer, my Provider, my Protector, and I couldn't be more thankful. Walking in to get my check up, I felt like I was walking on air. Where there was pain and insecurity before, there was confidence in the power of my Savior. The surgeon walked in and he immediately started to ask me how I felt. I told him that I felt great!

Then the conversation shifted to the results of the biopsy. He told me that my biopsy report was very short and that is something to be very thankful for in my case. He called me in to check on me and to let me know that the tumor was benign. I did not have cancer. I did not know my heart could become even more full than before, but it did. The surgeon then went on to explain how he did not know how my tumor on the left could have disappeared. He started to kind of ramble off to himself, maybe to come up with a scientific explanation of how a tumor could be so obviously there and then gone when it comes to the day for it to be removed. I looked at him before he could even say anything and said, "It is a miracle, I serve a great God." He looked at me and did not say anything but smiled and nodded. He continued to talk to my mom about various different technical details of how I should be feeling, when I could dance again, etc. The surgeon then gave me his card and told me that I could call him if I needed anything or if experienced any certain type of pain. I told him thank you.

Walking out of the office, I just looked up at the bright blue sky and whispered, "Thank you." I knew that there was no scientific explanation; there was no way someone could deny the power of my Savior. On the way back home, I sat in the car re-playing my past few months back in my mind. I got into a car accident that caused us to find the tumors in the first place. Then, time after time God sent people to encourage me which allowed me to know that He is with me and He has a greater purpose, all the way to this moment where I still have one healthy left ovary and how I will still be able to have children and do not have cancer. I never felt so alive. God proved himself to me and I could never deny His wonderful presence.

Chapter Nine: Power in Prayer

Chapter Ten

God Winks

The challenges I have faced were impossible to do alone. The prayers I have prayed were too bold for it to be just coincidence. Many of us have stories of hardships we have faced and have overcome. I challenge you to share them! Share all that Christ has done in your life.

Christ placed you through your trial or circumstance, but gave you a path through it. You are a living testimony of what you have been through personally. No one can share how greatly Jesus has impacted your life the way you can. I challenge you to place on your spiritual glasses and seek to see what God's purpose is. Find Him. God is the great I Am. I promise you, He is there, but you have to find Him.

Some of you are facing a trial right now and don't understand how it could ever work for good. You have read this, seen the hope I have found, and don't know if it is possible for the Lord to do the same in your life. Let me wipe any doubt away from your mind. It is possible for God. You may not be able to get through what you are facing alone, but that is just it. You aren't meant to go through it alone. Cling to the Lord. God is waiting for you with open arms and wants to reveal Himself to you. He may have already revealed Himself and you did not see it. I encourage you to look back at your life and find God in it.

Matthew 6:22-23 says, "The eye is the lamp of the body. So, if your eye is healthy, your whole body will be full of light, but if your eye is bad, your whole body will be full of darkness. If then the light in you is darkness, how great is the darkness!" I encourage you to check your eyes. Check to see if you can find how God has impacted your life. If you can't find where God has impacted your life, move past your eyes and search your heart. Ask yourself the bare and raw question, "If I can't see God moving in my life, did I ever accept Christ as my own?"

You may already know you have never accepted Christ as your personal Lord and Savior. You may have never been presented with the gospel. I pray that you choose to accept Jesus Christ as your personal Lord and Savior today. There is no greater day than today to do it. Once your heart is fixed upon the Lord, your eyes will have changed and I guarantee the Lord is working in your life.

In certain situations in life, it seems as if nothing good can come of them. I have heard and talked to various people who have gone through immense battles in their lives. They use that battle as an excuse to not come to Jesus. Well, I am not perfect. I am far from it. But I also know that I have questioned God myself. I never could have imagined that God could work out something so evil for good. It is possible. Give your life to Christ. Listen to Him. He may be trying to reveal to you the purpose of your hurt or the good that could possibly come from it.

I believe when God reveals the purpose or His grand picture behind His actions, it is God's way of winking at us. I went through an awful nightmare for three years and it wasn't until five years later that God revealed the purpose through it all. When He did, I believe it was God winking at me. Sometimes, God provides and answers right away, like with my friend in England. In only three days, I was able to rejoice in the Lord's plan. I saw Him winking yet again.

In each of our lives, there is something. Something that we are trying to keep from the cross. Leave it all at the cross. You are carrying an unnecessary burden and placing it upon your life. The Lord is there looking at you and saying, "My child, come to me. I will give you rest." Go to Him. Give Him everything, and when you do, leave it there. Leave your burden at the cross.

Then, take each day to grow closer to Him. At the peak of your life, take the time and say, 'God you are good.' Write it down somewhere, what you feel to be the ultimate low. Look back at the moments you were at the peak. Write down where you saw God move, where you saw God winking.

Remember that He is still good. Then, write down that struggle.

After your trial is over, I can't tell you how long it will be. It may be minutes, days, weeks, or years, but when He reveals His purpose, date the trial. Date the trial and note that is the day that God winked at you. God winks at each of us, we just have to take the time to see it.

Take the time to stop and find God in your life today.

This is Why

This is Why

About the Author
Jillian Murphy

Jillian Murphy is the founder of Radiant Ministries. Radiant Ministries is Jillian's platform dedicated to encourage people through scripture and persistent prayer to live lives to convince others to trust Christ. Also, Jillian is a Best-Selling author of the co-author book "A Bigger Purpose" as well as a professional speaker for Mike Rodriguez International, LLC.

Jillian's long-term goal is to establish a women's safe house on the foundation of Jesus Christ, and having a free health clinic as an extension of the safe house. In order to make this dream a reality, Jillian started her freshman year at a Christian University in Oklahoma, pursuing a degree in nursing in 2016. Jillian felt her call to ministry the Summer of 2014 on a mission trip in Washington D.C.

She followed God's plan for her life by interning at a women's safe house in Dallas, TX, Restored Hope Ministries, starting in the Fall of 2014. Jillian published her first book "The Four Seasons of Hope" July 2016. She wrote this book while still in high school. She continues to have a passion to use her writing to proclaim God's name. Jillian has used this passion to write "A Bigger Purpose" and "This is Why" during her freshman year of college.

Jillian has fallen in love with speaking to women. She talks about the seasons of life we are in as Christians and the why behind our difficult circumstances. Her favorite part of speaking is being able to pour all that she has learned into those around. Jillian believes that we are all like cups, we should be filled with scripture and by someone who can mentor us, while simultaneously pouring out into others that we mentor, so that the name of Jesus is proclaimed.

Everyone faces hardships and difficult circumstances in life that may seem impossible. Jillian believes that we can praise the God we serve through it all. At our lowest, at our peak, and everything in between if you have accepted Christ as your Lord and Savior, we already are victorious, now we need to act like it.

Jillian is the daughter of Dr. Tony L. Murphy and Michelle Murphy and has three siblings. Jillian's ultimate goal is to keep pointing others towards Christ, and continuously prays "less of me and more You, Lord." Her ultimate goal is to keep spreading the good news of Jesus Christ, while trying to live her life as a reflection of Him.

She is thankful for all God has done in her life and prays that she will continue to follow God's will in the future. Jillian's goal is to pursue writing more books, speaking to people about Jesus, and to impact lives in the name of Jesus. Jillian is available to speak at any size event, if you are interested in having Jillian come, please use the contact information below. Stay tuned for Jillian's journey!

Contact Jillian Murphy:

www.jillianmurphy.org

This is Why

This is Why

This is Why

Disclaimer & Copyright Information

Some of the events, locales, and conversations have been recreated from memories. In order to maintain their anonymity, in some instances, the names of individuals and places have been changed. As such, some identifying characteristics and details may have changed.

Although the author and publisher have made every effort to ensure that the information in this book was correct at press time, the author and publisher do not assume and hereby disclaim any liability to any party for any loss, damage, or disruption caused by errors or omissions, whether such errors or omissions result from negligence, accident, or any other cause.

All quotes, unless otherwise noted,
are attributed to the respective Author or to the Holy Bible.

Cover illustration, book design and production
Copyright © 2017 by Tribute Publishing, LLC
www.TributePublishing.com

Scripture references are copyrighted by www.BibleGateway.com
which is operated by the Zondervan Corporation, L.L.C.

This is Why

This is Why

This is Why

NOTES

This is Why

NOTES

CPSIA information can be obtained
at www.ICGtesting.com
Printed in the USA
BVOW08s0522070717
488543BV00001B/19/P